Union Cavalrymen
of the Civil War

Philip Katcher • Illustrated by Richard Hook

This American edition first published in 2003 by Raintree, a division of
Reed Elsevier Inc., Chicago, Illinois, by arrangement with Osprey Publishing
Limited, Oxford, England.

For information, address the publisher:
Raintree, 100 N. LaSalle, Suite 1200, Chicago, IL 60602

First published 1995
Under the title *Warrior 13: Union Cavalryman 1861–1865*
By Osprey Publishing Limited, Elms Court, Chapel Way, Botley,
Oxford, OX2 9LP
© 1995 Osprey Publishing Limited
All rights reserved.

ISBN 1-4109-0115-7

03 04 05 06 07   10 9 8 7 6 5 4 3 2 1

Library of Congress Cataloging-in-Publication Data

Katcher, Philip R. N.
  [Union cavalryman, 1861-1865]
  Union cavalrymen of the Civil War / Philip Katcher.
    v. cm. -- (A soldier's life)
  Originally published: Union cavalryman, 1861-1865. Oxford [England] :
Osprey, 1995, in series: Warrior.
  Includes bibliographical references and index.
  Contents: Historical background -- Enlistment -- Training -- Uniforms
and equipment -- Weapons -- Field service -- Combat & tactics -- Wounds
and sickness.
  ISBN 1-4109-0115-7 (library binding-hardcover)
  1. United States. Army. Cavalry--History--Civil War,
1861-1865--Juvenile literature. 2. Soldiers--United
States--History--19th century--Juvenile literature. 3. United
States--History--Civil War, 1861-1865--Cavalry operations--Juvenile
literature. [1. United States. Army. Cavalry--History. 2.
Soldiers--History--19th century. 3. United States--History--Civil War,
1861-1865--Cavalry operations.] I. Title. II. Series.
  E492.5.K38 2003
  973.7'41--dc21
                          2003005313

Author: Philip Katcher
Illustrator: Richard Hook
Printed in China through World Print Ltd.

Author's dedication
This book is dedicated to the memory of my great uncle, Sergeant Byron Kear
of Co. D, 144th Ohio National Guard.

Artist's note
Readers may care to note that the original paintings from which the color
plates in this book were prepared are available for private sale. All reproduction
copyright whatsoever is retained by the Publishers. All enquiries should be
addressed to:

Scorpio Gallery
PO Box 475
Hailsham
East Sussex
BN27 2SH

CONTENTS

UNION CAVALRYMEN OF THE CIVIL WAR

HISTORICAL BACKGROUND

In December 1860, when South Carolina seceded from the Union, the regular US Army contained only five mounted regiments. Considering the vast size of the United States (and of the new Confederate States of America, as the Southern states soon styled themselves), this was a wholly inadequate cavalry with which to fight a war. In addition to the five regular regiments, only a handful of volunteer cavalry companies existed: infantry had been preferred, due to the high cost of equipping and maintaining mounted units.

The 1st Regiment of Dragoons had been raised in 1836; the 2nd Regiment of Dragoons had originally been raised as a mounted rifle regiment,

and redesignated in 1844. The Regiment of Mounted Riflemen dated from 1846. The 1st and 2nd Cavalry Regiments had been raised in 1855, under Secretary of War Jefferson Davis, who would become the President of the Confederacy. Seeing the need for more mounted troops to fight the Civil War, Congress authorized a 3rd Cavalry Regiment in May 1861; it was actually organized in Pittsburgh, Pennsylvania, on June 18, 1861. To bring these six assorted mounted units under tighter and more uniform control, all were redesignated Cavalry

This is what recruits thought they were getting into the cavalry for – a full-blown, saber-waving charge which would roll over the enemy like a breaking wave. The reality was to be quite different.

Regiments on August 3, 1861: the 1st Dragoons became the new 1st Cavalry, and the other units were redesignated in the order of seniority as the 2nd, 3rd, 4th, 5th, and 6th Cavalry Regiments.

Since it was clearly apparent that six cavalry regiments would not be enough to serve on a front that stretched for a thousand miles, the US Army's Adjutant General, Lorenzo Thomas, asked officially for the raising of 40,000 cavalrymen on February 19, 1862. Henceforward, each state's governor was asked to raise a few volunteer units of cavalry as well as infantry and artillery. The numbers requested were not large: the Federal government was unable to equip large numbers of cavalry. Indeed, when the war broke out the government only had 4,076 cavalry carbines, 27,192 pistols, 16,933 sabers, and 4,320 sets of horse equipment, most of which were required for the regular regiments. In all it took

some $500,000 – $600,000 to equip a single caval[ry] regiment, on top of higher pay rates for officer[s] and the cost of recruiting other necessar[y] professionals such as saddlers and blacksmiths.

The basic unit of organization of the cavalry wa[s] the regiment. According to General Order 1[4] dated May 4, 1861, a cavalry regiment was to hav[e] three battalions, each with two squadrons, each [of] two companies. A regiment had a minimu[m] strength on paper of 997 officers and enlisted me[n].

The following figures give some idea of the rat[e] of expansion of the cavalry. On December 31, 186[1] the cavalry strength of the Union numbered 4,74[?] in the regular army, as well as another 54,65[?] volunteers. By June 30, 1862, this had grown to 7[?] cavalry regiments totaling 71,196 men. Th[e] Assistant Chief of Cavalry reported on August [6] 1863, that the US Army mustered 174 caval[ry] regiments with 109,126 men. As of February 1[?] 1865, the Cavalry Bureau reported that there wer[e] 160,237 cavalrymen on its rolls, of which 105,43[?] were present and fit for duty. 154,000 horses ha[d] been purchased in the previous year, and ther[e] were 77,847 horses which were considere[d] serviceable. The Cavalry Bureau was organized o[n] July 28, 1863, to take overall charge of th[e] organization, equipment, and horses. Maj. Ge[n.] George Stoneman was its first chief, replaced b[y] Brig. Gen. J. H. Wilson on January 26, 1864.

ENLISTMENT

The bombardment by Confederate artillery of Fo[rt] Sumter on April 12, 1861, was the spark that final[ly] set off the Civil War, and quickly brought thousan[ds] of eager volunteers for the Union cause. It prove[d] especially easy to raise cavalry, since recruits naive[ly] believed that their military duties would be easi[er] than in the infantry, and that they would be able [to] ride to war instead of having to walk. Few, howeve[r] were aware of the arduous chores inseparable fro[m]

There were a handful of pre-war militia cavalry units, mostly i[n] larger cities, and recruited from volunteers with enough mon[ey] to afford a horse, equipment, and fancy uniforms. This man is a member of Philadelphia's First City Troop, which had been founded in 1775 and saw Revolutionary War service. His uniform style, however, dates from the War of 1812. (Author's collection)

he care of cavalry horses. One Union officer later admitted that before the war he thought the typical cavalryman "was a swashbuckler, who rode terrifically with a saber gripped by his teeth, a revolver in each hand, and his breath almost aflame as it spurted from his nostrils." Such illusions were quickly dispelled by the realities of war.

To raise as large a body of volunteers as quickly as possible, local civic leaders and other suitable men were empowered to raise a company, or occasionally a regiment. The new officers then spread out into the countryside to find volunteers to fill out their units.

"The method of obtaining enlistments was to hold war meetings in schoolhouses," wrote an Ohio cavalry officer. "The recruiting officer, accompanied by a good speaker, would attend an evening meeting which had been duly advertised. The latter did the talking, the former was ready with blanks to obtain signatures and administer the oath." Though these meetings were generally well attended, "sometimes it was difficult to induce anybody to volunteer."

The government set a strict minimum for the size of a newly recruited company before it was accepted onto government payrolls and its officers received their official commissions. These minimums applied even to existing volunteer cavalry units organized, uniformed, and equipped long before the war began.

One pre-war volunteer unit, from just outside Washington City, volunteered for service in June 1861 and was accepted. But, according to one of its members, "there was still an obstacle in the way. The government would not muster a man unless a fully organized company, with a minimum aggregate of seventy-nine men, were presented to the mustering officer. Captain Wister and his [troops] rode all over the country, among the farmers' sons, in quest of recruits; but all his efforts failed to raise the requisite number of men who were able and willing to find their own horses and equipments, notwithstanding that the government had offered to pay the troopers forty cents per day

A number of volunteer cavalry units wore special variations of the regulation dress. The 3rd New Jersey Cavalry, who designated themselves the 1st US Hussars, wore the most elaborate variation, with orange collar tabs and rows of yellow tape across the jacket front. (Richard Carlile Collection)

Corporal Windsor B. Smith, a 5ft. 9in. tall resident of Portland, Maine, joined Co. K, 1st Maine Cavalry Regiment, on August 21, 1862. In January 1863 he was detached from the company to serve as an orderly to Brig. Gen. Gabriel Paul, who was blinded by a bullet in the first day's fighting at Gettysburg. Smith returned to the regiment and was appointed corporal. This photo was taken when he was on furlough at home in December 1863. He was further promoted to sergeant on May 1, 1864. He was captured on September 29, 1864, and paroled that July. His health was so damaged by his time in Confederate prison camps that he never regained his strength and was discharged in July 1865. (Author's collection)

for their use and risk; with the proviso, however, that, in case the trooper lost his horse in any way, he must furnish another, or serve on foot. This proviso was the straw that broke the camel's back. After three months spent in drilling, and in unavailing efforts to fill up, Captain Wister's troop disbanded, on [June 30], and its members sought service in their commands."

Despite these problems, the first call for volunteer forces was rapidly met. Although regulations demanded only physically fit men between the ages of 18 and 45, many volunteers who were unfit, too old or too young passed the cursory physical examination which doctors were required to give each recruit. This was despite th recommendation that "A cavalry soldier should n exceed in weight one hundred and sixty pound should be active and strong, physically sound, wit a natural fondness for horses and experience i handling them."

The Recruit

People looking at surviving period clothing tod often comment on the small stature of Civil W soldiers. This is something of an oversimplificatio In fact, over ten percent of the volunteers in e.g. th 1st Wisconsin Cavalry were over 6 ft. tall; whi Captain W.W. La Grange was 6 ft. 4 in. tall, the sam height as Abraham Lincoln. The average recruit w in his early twenties and American born, thoug most were only one or two generations remove from their European heritage, and there were larg numbers of German- and Irish-born citizens. In typical company – Co. C, 9th Pennsylvania Cavalr all but 17 men were born in Pennsylvania, whi seven came from Germany, three from Ireland, tw from England, and one from Wales.

Background was generally rural, and about ha of all Union Army recruits were farmers. Since th cavalry was seen as more glamorous than othe branches of service it appealed to the higher soci classes, and attracted a higher proportion of me from non-farming backgrounds than othe branches. The typical Union cavalry regime contained men from virtually every walk of life. Th 156 enlisted men of Co. C, 9th Pennsylvania Caval included representatives of 36 occupation including an artist, blacksmith, boatbuilde brickmaker, carpenter, chairmaker, chemis cigarmaker, engineer, engraver, farrier, gunsmit laborer, machinest, mason, merchant, mille miner, painter, physician, plasterer, printe railroader, saddler, tailor, teacher, teamster, ar weaver. In all, over 60 percent of the compan men had a profession, while only 20 percent sa they were farmers.

The recruits of the 1st Ohio Cavalry, by contra were said to have been mostly farmers' sons wh were also accustomed to riding and to handlir horse equipment. The 17th Pennsylvania Caval Regiment, formed in late 1862, was made u according to the regimental historian, mostly farmers, lumbermen and mechanics. "Fortunatel he noted, "most of them were good horsemen."

The dress jacket was to be worn, as here by a private of the 16th New York Cavalry Regiment, with brass shoulder scales and the dress hat, often called the "Hardee" or "Jeff Davis" hat. The gloves were not an issue item, although most men tried to get a pair, especially in colder weather. (Richard Carlile Collection)

Not everyone, however, was impressed with the quality of Union cavalry recruits. One bitter New York cavalry officer commented: "No one can have been with our cavalry long, and observed carefully the material of which these regiments are made up, without being struck with their great inferiority, mentally and physically, when compared with either the infantry or artillery."

After the first volunteer units had been enlisted, company-grade officers were elected; it was generally the case that local civic leaders received these posts. Some regiments were fortunate enough to recruit veterans of the Mexican War or the 1848 revolutions in Europe, and these men were natural choices for officers. Most new officers, however, had to learn their trade alongside their men. Colonels were usually appointed by state governors, and were often professionals technically "on leave" from their regular army assignments in order to serve in a volunteer regiment. When experienced soldiers or professionals were not available, however, officers were simply chosen from among men who were seen to have a flair for command or were respected members of society, though some most unlikely sounding candidates were chosen. "We elected our own officers," wrote a 3rd Colorado Cavalry Regiment veteran. "Hal Sayre, a mining superintendent, was elected to be captain. H.B. Orahood, a druggist at Central City, was elected first lieutenant; and Harry Richmond, a tragedian with Languish and Atwater's theatrical troupe, second lieutenant. Late that fall, just before we were ready to start from Bijou Basin, Hal Sayre was promoted to major and Orahood was made captain." Eventually the army had to set up panels to screen its volunteer officers, and remove the worst of them from their commissions.

The first cavalrymen found the war far rougher than they had anticipated, as indeed did all Federal troops. Losses were high, both in killed and permanently disabled. Once news of the ugly realities of war filtered through to the civilian community it grew harder to find volunteers; eventually large cash bounties had to be offered to tempt recruits. This money succeeded in enticing some men: "It was in 1864 that I joined a cavalry regiment in the department of the Gulf, a raw recruit in a veteran regiment," wrote a member of the 4th Wisconsin Cavalry.

"It may be asked why I waited so long befor enlisting, and why I enlisted at all, when the war wa so near over. I know that most of the soldier enlisted from patriotic motives, and because the wanted to help shed blood, and wind up the war. did not. I enlisted for the bounty. I thought the wa was nearly over, and that the probabilities were tha the regiment I had enlisted in would be ordere home before I could get to it. In fact the recruitin officer told me as much, and he said I would get m bounty, and a few months' pay, and it would be ju: like finding money."

Some who joined for the bounty money deserte at the first chance, only to enlist elsewhere fo another bounty. Many states retained the bountie: at least in part, for payment upon discharge. Y enough money had to be paid in advance to brin in recruits – men could often earn more in civilia jobs than the $13 a month paid in the openin stages of the war to Union privates.

Even with the bounty system in place there wer not enough volunteers, and in 1863 a conscriptio law had to be passed. Conscripted men could sti avoid service by paying a fee or hiring a substitut to take their place, but the army was from this poir on largely able to maintain its forces at sufficier strength. Conscripts were, however, generally le: well motivated and often less physically able to serv than the early volunteers.

TRAINING

Even if cavalry recruits were already goo horsemen, which was not often the case, all of the still needed training. "Camps of Instruction" wer set up near larger towns, where railroads coul bring in the recruits and the supplies they woul need. The newly recruited companies, whe complete, were brought to these camps and forme into regiments. At the camp the recruit received h uniform, weapons, and equipment, though n always at once. "The process of mounting an

The dress jacket was also trimmed on the back with yellow tape. The fabric tabs at the bottom of each seam were called "belt support pillars" and were designed to keep the saber be from slipping off the jacket. In service, some soldiers opened the seams of these pillars and used them as hiding places for money in case of capture. (Author's collection)

Many dress jackets worn by volunteers had lower collars than those issued to regulars, with only one false buttonhole on each side. The crossed sabre cap badge was not regulation but was widely worn by cavalrymen, as by the man on the right here. (S. Shazo)

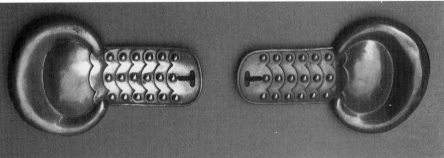

These shoulder scales show the rivets added to the non-commissioned officer's version.

equipping went on slowly," wrote a 1st New York Cavalry officer. "At one time we could get horses but no equipments; at another, equipments but no horses. Then sabers were not to be had, although it appeared as if everybody was offering to sell the Government sabers. Few, indeed, were the pistols to be had; and it was months before we could get a carbine."

The first task of the cavalry recruit was to learn how to care for his horse, and how to assemble the confusing tangle of saddlery and harness. He was then taught dismounted drill – the simple facing movements, marching, and saluting – before

proceeding to the more complicated mounte drill. Riding a horse into battle was quite differe from riding to church on Sunday. The army issue strict instructions on how training would k conducted:

"*The recruit commences his instruction on foot. T first week after his arrival at the regiment is employ exclusively in instructing him in all the details discipline, police, and interior service, and in tho relating to his dress and the grooming of his horse.*

"*He is taught to mount without saddle on both sides the horse. He is taught the name and use of the princip parts of the arms and equipments, and the manner keeping them clean; the manner of rolling the cloak, folding the effects, and of placing them in the valise. The different instructions are given by the corporal of t squad, under the superintendence of the sergeant ar officer of the platoon. At the end of this week, the recru commences the first lesson on foot; he continues to instructed in the above-mentioned details. The recruits a drilled on foot twice a day, when possible, an hour ea time. Their instruction on horseback is commenced at t same time with the saber exercise.*"

The soldier also had to learn by heart tl commands as transmitted by bugle, the battlefie being too noisy for voice commands. Thes commands, according to Cooke's Tactics, were:

"*1. The general. 2. Boots and saddles. 3. To horse. The assembly. 5. To arms. 6. To the standard. 7. T march (it also answers for a quick step on foot). 8. T charge. 9. The rally. 10. Reveille. 11. Stable call. 1 Watering call. 13. Breakfast call. 14. Assembly of t guard. 15. Orders for the orderly sergeants. 16. Assembl of the trumpeters. 17. Retreat. 18. Fatigue call. 1 Dinner call. 20. Distributions. 21. Drill call. 22. Office. call. 23. The recall 24. Sick call. 25. Tattoo. 26. extinguish lights.*"

As if these were not enough, a separate group bugle calls were set aside "For the service skirmishers":

"*1. Forward. 2. Halt. 3. To the left. 4. To the right. The about. 6. Change direction to the right. 7. Chan direction to the left. 8. Trot. 9. Gallop. 10. To commen firing. 11. To cease firing. 12. To charge as foragers. T rally is No. 9, general signals.*"

Non-commissioned officers, such as this sergeant, were authorized red worsted sashes. The yellow stripe down each leg has photographed black on the film of the day.

There was, however, always the problem of finding qualified personnel to train recruits. Most training was to have been conducted by corporals. According to Cooke's *Tactics*, "The Corporals should be capable of executing all the lessons mounted and dismounted, and should be qualified to teach the *school of the trooper dismounted*, and at least 4 lessons mounted." Sergeants were to perform the more advanced stages of training, and were, according to the manual, to be "capable of executing, dismounted and mounted, all that is prescribed by this book; and should be able to teach the lessons of the *school of the trooper*, and to command a platoon in the *school of the squadron mounted*."

Unfortunately, most sergeants and corporals of newly recruited companies knew as little about soldiering as the privates. New NCOs were forced to read the manuals, usually keeping one step ahead of their trainees by studying the next day's lesson the evening before. Usually each regiment had one or two old soldiers who had campaign experience in the Mexican War or had served in a pre-war volunteer company, and these held nightly classes for the new NCOs. There was no set program of training nor length of time allotted for it. Often, as soon as a regiment was formed it was sent to join the field army even if it lacked the necessary equipment. Training was then improvised in the field.

In April 1862 the 4th Pennsylvania Cavalry Regiment was sent on to Washington without horses, and was immediately threatened with conversion into infantry. To prevent this the commander concocted a wily scheme. He drew horses that were unfit for service on the pretext of training his men in the rudiments of mounting and riding. In the meantime some of his men had been assigned to the Provost Marshal's office, and were issued good horses for their duties. The commander exchanged these few good horses for some of the unfit nags. When the cavalry inspectors visited the regimental camp they immediately got the impression that the entire regiment was indeed mounted. The inspectors instructed that the worn-out nags be exchanged for good mounts from the artillery stables. Thus the regiment managed to remain a cavalry formation, and received some much-needed training into the bargain.

The 17th Pennsylvania Cavalry Regiment was formed in late 1862, and set up its training camp outside Harrisburg, Pennsylvania. "In this camp horses, sabers and horse equipments were issued, and the active duties of the soldier commenced," the regimental historian wrote. "Drill, drill, drill, drill was now the order over and over again. Drill by squads! drill by company! drill by squadron! drill by regiment! Then there were dress parades, guard,

...llow chevrons on each arm marked non–commissioned officers. ...his man wears an unofficial chevron which first appeared ...ound May 1863: the one bar and three chevrons represent a ...mpany quartermaster sergeant. (Richard Carlile Collection)

fatigue and other camp duties of various kinds, which kept the men almost constantly employed. At first these drills and camp duties were cheerfully accepted by the men, but soon they became monotonous and were regarded by some as superfluous and unnecessary ... Then there were dismounted drills, saber drills, carbine drills, revolver drills, and various other drills. Considerable stress was given to the saber drill, that being the chief weapon used when on duty, dress parade and review occasions. The colonel established a school of instruction, and the officers were obliged to make themselves thoroughly acquainted with the tactics and other military duties."

There was, however, no formal schooling available for officers either. In some regiments officers were expected to pick up the necessary skills by observation and reading on their own. I others, especially where the regimental commande had prior military experience, officers took evenin classes on topics such as army regulations, caval tactics and requisition procedures. When the 1 New York Cavalry was first formed, according to on member, its commander opened schools instruction, "and the officers applied themselves t the tactics. We had company drills, too, nearly ever day, but the work of training new horses so that the could execute movements with celerity progresse slowly. Efficiency was a thing not to be attained in month or even a year; nor was it difficult to see fror the slow progress we made in improvement what Herculean task it was to make an army a gener could feel safe with in the face of an enemy."

Other regiments arranged more specialize training for their men. In the 1st New Jerse Cavalry's training camp, according to its chaplair "several times the regiment was ordered out as if f the march, until the men became accustomed t pack and saddle well and promptly."

The men who joined in 1861 were the luck ones: they at least received some preliminar training before being sent out on active campaign In later years new recruits were forwarded direct to their regiments, without any stay at a camp instruction. There they had to "learn the rope with only the friendly help of the more experience troopers and NCOs. Some progressive regimen set up "Q" troops, in which recruits received th basic training. Eventually, however, most regimen lost so many trained men and had such a hig proportion of recruits they had to virtually begi anew. The 2nd New York Cavalry, for example, w down to some 350 all ranks by the end of th Second Bull Run campaign; this was one of number of regiments from the Army of th Potomac which returned to the outskirts Washington to set up a new camp of instruction fc their recruits.

Again, some back-to-basics training was given i the winter of 1863–64 when a new tactical system fc

Battalion quartermaster sergeants, like this man, wore two bars over their three chevrons. His otherwise plain dark blue jacket is trimmed around the top and front of the collar and down the front with yellow tape. This was common among Pennsylvania cavalrymen.

valry was introduced. "There was little time for st or recreation," wrote one Michigan veteran. .ong and tiresome drills and 'schools of struction' made up the daily routine. In one spect, however, these drills of troops, regiment d brigade were a good thing. Many hundreds of ew recruits were sent on from Michigan and, eing put in with the old men, they were worked to good soldiers before the campaign opened, d proved to be as reliable and efficient as the terans with whom they were associated."

In much the same way, when Maj. Gen. James H. ilson was given a corps of cavalry in the Western eater in the winter of 1864, he made sure that "a orough system of instruction for men and officers s instituted, and every necessary effort was made bring the corps to the highest possible state of ficiency." This, unlike much previous training, nphasized dismounted tactics, especially using the uick-loading seven-shot Spencer carbine, which ve Wilson's troops far greater firepower than any otential enemy. In reality, the average cavalryman arned how to perform his duties more from rvice in the field than from formal training rograms.

In many ways, the objective of all military aining is to turn a man into an obedient utomaton. In this respect the Civil War training iled. As a New York cavalry officer later noted, he American solider is an observing, thinking eing. You can never destroy his individuality; you n not make him a mere piece of machinery. He s a rough and homely way of criticizing what is bing on around him, but his criticisms are well ken, and tersely expressed. He observes the ovement of his general closely, obeys his orders ecause it is his duty, but respects him only so far as s ability entitles him to respect."

NIFORMS AND QUIPMENT

n August 17, 1861, Captain William E. Doster, Co. 4th Pennsylvania Cavalry Regiment, put in his st requisition for the basic uniforms and

equipment needed to equip his newly organized company of 92 enlisted men. For each he requested: a complete cavalry cap, a blouse, a coat [i.e. dress jacket], one pair of trousers, two flannel shirts, two pairs of underwear, two pairs of stockings, a pair of boots, a great coat, a blanket, a haversack and a canteen complete with straps. In addition he also requested two wall tents complete with flies, poles, and pins, 17 "common tents," 12 spades, 12 axes, four pickaxes, 12 hatchets, 12 camp kettles, 30 mess pans, a sash [probably for the company's first, or orderly, sergeant], two bugles with cords and tassels, a "descriptive book," an "order book," a "clothing book," and a morning report book. This list gives an idea of the equipment of an individual trooper, and all the additional items necessary to equip a single company.

rriers often adopted an unofficial badge of a saddler's knife. is man also has a pair of issue spurs on his boots. (Richard rlile Collection)

Cavalryman's dress

The US Army was one of the first to have both a fatigue dress and a full dress. The Union cavalryman's full dress headgear was a stiff, broad-brimmed hat, turned up on one side; these hats were generally detested as being worthless and were rarely worn after the first few months; indeed many units threw them away at the first opportunity. The dark blue short jacket, trimmed with yellow braid, was better liked and was often even worn as a fatigue item. Trousers were dark blue until December 1861, when the color was changed to a cheaper sky blue. They were reinforced with a double thickness of cloth on the inside of the leg to prolong wear. Laced bootees were issued, though many soldiers purchased knee-length boots of their own, and these were sometimes issued as well.

The fatigue dress included a dark blue cap with a leather peak which was based on a floppy version of the pre-war dress shako. Officially, for enlisted men, it was to bear the regimental number only but this tended to be accompanied by a crossed saber badge as a mark of the cavalry branch. The fatigue tunic, known as a blouse, was also dark blue. It reached to below the hip bone like a modern suit jacket, was fastened in front with four brass buttons, and had an inside pocket over the left breast. The same trousers were worn for full dress and fatigue use.

Winter wear for enlisted men included a double-breasted sky blue overcoat with a standing collar and a cape that reached to the cuffs. NCOs' chevrons were worn on the lower sleeves just above the cuffs, so that they were visible while the cape was being worn loose around the shoulders.

In the field and on fatigue duties in camp, officers were authorized waist-length jackets. These were quite popular, since frock coats were less comfortable when the wearer was mounted. The jackets were usually cut single-breasted, regardless of the wearer's rank, although some field officers did wear double-breasted jackets. For winter use officers wore a dark blue double-breasted overcoat; toward the end of the war officers were allowed to wear enlisted men's overcoats, to make them less of a target in the field. (For additional information on uniform items, insignia of rank, etc., see Battle Ready: *Civil War Union Troops.*)

Cavalry officers often embellished their uniforms with non-regulation touches. Brig. Gen. George A. Custer, commanding the Michigan Brigade, was seen by a brigade member in July 1863: "He was clad in a suit of black velvet, elaborately trimmed with gold lace, which ran down the outer seams of his trousers, and almost covered the sleeves of his cavalry jacket. The wide collar of a blue navy shirt was turned down over the collar of his velvet jacket.

This standard issue fatigue dress has been decorated by the addition of a colored collar and tape down the front and on each cuff. An outside left breast pocket has also been added. Photographed in St. Louis, site of an important cavalry post, this soldier was a member of the 16th Illinois Cavalry.

nd a necktie of brilliant crimson was tied in a knot
the throat, the long ends falling in front. The
ouble rows of buttons on his breast were arranged
n groups of two, indicating the rank of a brigadier
eneral. A soft, black hat with wide brim adorned
ith a gilt cord, and rosette encircling a silver star,
as turned down on one side giving him a rakish
r." While Custer was a noted dandy, many officers
xercised a less dazzling degree of sartorial latitude:
is was, after all, an army in which regulars were far
utnumbered by duration-only citizen soldiers.

Enlisted men also often preferred to wear other
an issue clothing. Many did not like the yellow-
ced jackets, preferring instead plain dark blue
ckets made to their own specifications. These
ere mostly single-breasted, with a slash breast
ocket over the left breast and a short standing
ollar. A Wisconsin volunteer in 1864 had just such
plain jacket made for him when he joined, but
ter a period of hard service it wore out and he had
draw an issue uniform: "I can remember now
ow my heart sank within me, as I picked up a pair
pants that was left. They were evidently cut out
ith a buzz-saw, and were made for a man that
eighed 300 pounds ... The sergeant charged the
nts to my account, and then handed me a jacket,
small one, evidently made for a hump-backed
warf. The jacket was covered with yellow braid. O,
yellow, that it made me sick. The jacket was
arged to me, also. Then he handed me some
dershirts and drawers, so coarse and rough that
seemed to me that they must have been made of
pe, and lined with sand-paper. Then came an
ercoat, big enough for an equestrian statue of
eorge Washington, with a cape on it as big as a
ll tent. The hat I drew was a stiff, cheap, shoddy
t, as high as a tin camp kettle, which was to take
e place of my nobby, soft felt hat I had paid five
ollars of my bounty money for. The hat was four
zes too large for me. Then I took the last pair of
my shoes there was, and they weighed as much as
pair of anvils, and had raw-hide strings to fasten
em with. Has any old soldier of the army ever

forgotten the clothing that he drew from the
quartermaster? These inverted pots for hats, the
same size all the way up, and the shoes that seemed
to be made of sole leather, and which scraped the
skin off the ankles. O, if this government ever does
go to Gehenna [Hell], as some people content it
will sometime, it will be as a penalty for issuing such
ill-fitting shoddy clothing to its brave soldiers."

Many enlisted cavalrymen wore pieces of civilian
and even Confederate dress. As late as July 31, 1864,
officers of the veteran 2nd Iowa Cavalry Regiment
had to be ordered that, "The regiment having been
supplied with clothing, no article of citizen's

the field mounted men, including officers, often wore
stom-made versions of the fatigue blouse which were longer
an usual and featured several outside pockets. Regimental
uartermaster Sergeant Robert G. Huston, 118th Illinois
ounted Infantry, also wears the kind of broad-brimmed hat
ich was another popular personal acquisition, especially in
e West. (Richard Tibbals)

15

The issue enlisted man's overcoat had a cape that reached the cuffs, and two rows of buttons down the front. In the rush to get uniforms to the men in 1861, materials other than the regulation sky blue wool often had to be used for these coats, as in this dark blue example. (David Scheinmann)

Non-commissioned officers, such as First Sergeant Elbridge Williams, pictured here, wore chevrons on their overcoat cuff so they would not be hidden by their capes. Note the boots with flaps that covered the knee. These were not issued, but bought from sutlers or sent from home. (Richard Carlile Collection)

apparel whatever will be allowed to be worn. All such clothing in possession of the men must be disposed of today. Company officers will make a minute inspection of their Company quarters and the men's knapsacks tomorrow morning, and all hats, coats, and pants other than the prescribed uniform will be taken possession of and burned."

The fact is, however, that no amount of orders could stop the men – and even the officers – from wearing wide-brimmed black civilian hats in the field. The superior quality of most civilian items ensured that they remained popular with the men throughout the war. Indeed, on July 5, 1864, the men of the 2nd Michigan even had to be ordered not to wear "the whole or part of the confederate

uniform." One can understand why th Confederate uniform, especially in the hot Sout would be preferred to the US Army issue dres many Southern summer garments were made denim or cotton cloth, while the US Army unifor issued year-round, was made entirely of wool.

Heavy gloves, often cut with large gauntlet cuf were useful when riding. Strangely, these were n issued, and both officers and men had to buy the from sutlers or get them sent from home. Most we made of natural buff leather, though some office

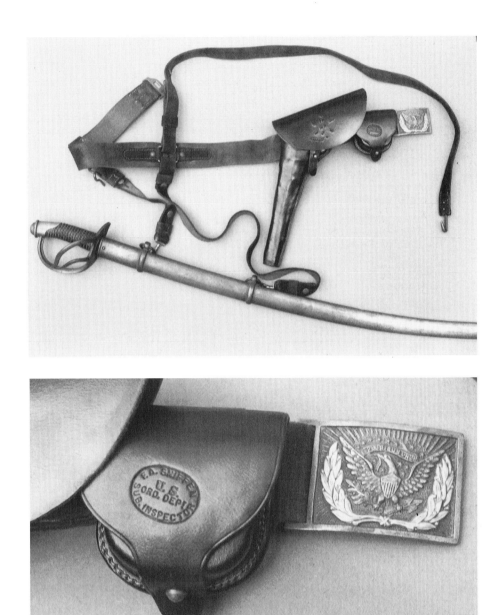

The basic enlisted cavalryman's belt had two slings to hang the saber from the left side, while the pistol and cap pouch were worn on the right. A sling that passed over the right shoulder helped support the weight of the sword; this was disliked and was often discarded.

A close-up of the belt plate showing the separate silver wreath applied to the cast brass belt plate. The percussion cap box has US Army Ordnance Department inspector's markings.

and the cuffs embroidered with a gold eagle, stars, the national motto or some similar design.

Equipment

The equipment included a sword belt with a rectangular brass belt plate featuring a spread-winged eagle enclosed by a silver wreath. The belt was generally made of buff leather, dark brown on the outside and left a natural cream color on the inside, although it rapidly grew the same color inside and out after a short period of wear. The saber hung on the left hip, and a black pistol holster on the right

hip. A small leather pouch for percussion caps was normally worn on the right just in front of the holster to allow easy access to it when using the carbine: however, in order to get all the necessary pouches on the belt, the cap box was just as often worn on the front left hip. The cap pouch had a piece of sheepskin placed just inside to prevent caps from falling out when it was left open, as often occurred in combat. It also contained a nipple pick, a thin piece of iron wire used to clean out the nipple of the carbine or pistol, which often fouled up during use. A slightly larger pouch for pistol ammunition was worn behind the holster. Enlisted men also carried carbines, slung by a spring and swivel hook from a wide belt, with a large brass frame buckle, around the body. The larger carbine ammunition pouch was often worn on the carbine belt, unless the cap box were worn on the left side, in which case it could be crammed onto the sword belt.

A wool-covered canteen was slung from the saddle or worn around the body, along with a waterproofed haversack in which the man's rations, and spare ammunition, were to be carried. Each man also received a pair of spurs (although these were often purchased privately, particularly by officers); and necessary horse equipment. This was based around the Army's issue McClellan saddle, named for its deviser Maj. Gen. George B. McClellan, who had copied it from European models. The other equipment included saddle bags, a picket pin, a rope, a feed bag for the horse, and a "boot" in which to rest the carbine muzzle.

WEAPONS

The cavalry was the best armed of all the branches of service. The cavalryman's sword, intended for mounted combat, was either the M1840 heavy cavalry saber or the similar but lighter version designed in 1860. Both were based on an earlier French model and featured a slightly curved blade, a brass guard, and a leather handgrip bound with twisted wire. The sword was carried in an iron scabbard, and usually had a brown leather sabe knot attached to the guard; this was worn aroun the wrist in action, preventing the saber from bein dropped.

Sabers and knives

Sabers were normally issued with blunt blades. I the summer of 1862 a Georgia regiment of th Confederate cavalry notified the men of the 7 Pennsylvania Cavalry Regiment that they ha sharpened their sabers and were planning to sho the Federal cavalry what sabers were intended fo Soon afterwards the 7th captured several Georgia and found that their sabers had, indeed, bee sharpened. The Pennsylvanians immediately pt their own sabers to the grindstone – fortunately, it turned out. In a battle soon afterwards the 7 Pennsylvania charged with drawn sabers, clearin the facing Confederate line within five minutes fo the loss of only 45 men.

Besides belt knives, which many men carried, th other major edged weapon, the lance, was use only by a single regiment and for a relatively bri period. Maj. Gen. George B. McClella commander of the Army of the Potomac, ha before the war visited a number of European armi and had been impressed by their lancer formation In November 1861 he suggested that one of h cavalry regiments should be converted to lancer and the 6th Pennsylvania was chosen.

In the event, the lance did not live up expectations. One veteran recalled that, "Ou

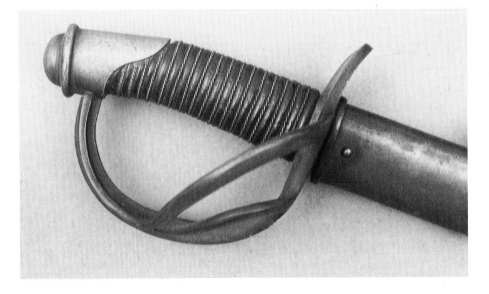

The hilt of the M1840 dragoon saber, the "old wristbreaker." The M186 light cavalry saber was quite similar in appearance.

eapon being unfitted for any service but the harge, we were held only to resist attack from the nemy." A Southern cavalryman later recalled how Rush's Lancers" were attacked by Confederate avalry, "but before our Virginia horsemen got ithin fifty yards of their line, this magnificent egiment, which had doubtless excited the liveliest dmiration in Northern cities, turned tail and fled a disorder, strewing the whole line of their retreat ith their picturesque but inconvenient arms. The ntire skirmish, if such it may be called, was over in ss time than it is required to record it: and I do not elieve that out of the whole body of 700 men, more han twenty retained their lances." In 1863, ecognizing the uselessness of the lance in North merica, the 6th turned in their remaining weapons o the quartermaster stores, and replaced them with e more conventional Spencer carbines and pistols.

istols

he pistol was a far more popular weapon. Six-shot evolvers made by Colt Firearms Co. were the most ommon; other models made by such companies as avage and Starr appeared in far smaller numbers han the Colts. The issue "Army" Colt pistol was 44 caliber, although 0.36 caliber "Navy" models ere also popular, especially among officers, who referred their lighter weight. They fired paper-rapped cartridges, using copper percussion caps o ignite the charge. The revolver, though valued or a quick firing rate, was not yet a refined weapon: ercussion caps would sometimes fly apart on ring, causing the revolving cylinder to jam; and

there was always the danger that a single shot might set off all six rounds at once, with crippling effect. Pistols were accurate only at very short range, which meant they were useful only in cavalry mêlées and other close actions, which were not particularly common.

Carbines

The most useful cavalry weapon was the carbine. Most were manufactured by private companies; Union troopers were issued with a plethora of designs, some good and some bad. The breechloading carbine was standard, but the types can be classed as firing either fixed ammunition or paper ammunition, the latter being the most common, especially in the early stages of the war. Carbines were both shorter and smaller in bore than the 0.58 or 0.577 caliber rifle muskets of the infantry; most were between 0.50 and 0.54 caliber.

The Sharps carbine was initially the most popular model. It used a paper or linen cartridge box, inserted in the breech through a falling block that sheared off the paper when closed. A 0.52 caliber weapon, it weighed 7fl pounds and was 39 inches long. One reason for its popularity was its simple mechanism, which worked well no matter how dirty it got from mud or gunpowder residue.

The side of the Smith carbine showing the ring which was used to hook the carbine to the carbine sling. The owner of this particular carbine, Sergeant Franklin Thomas, Co. A, 12th Illinois Cavalry Regiment, carved his name on the stock, as can still be seen. (Chris Nelson)

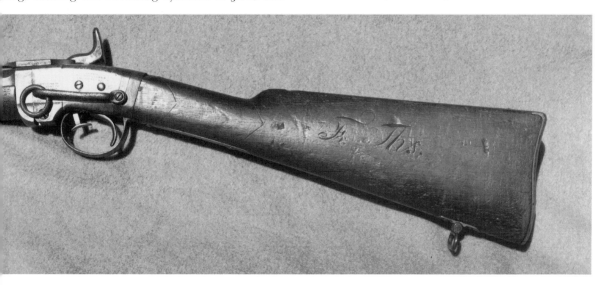

This cavalryman holds his new M1859 Sharps carbine and M1860 light cavalry saber, complete with black leather saber knot. He has two M1851 Colt Navy revolvers stuck in his belt. His broad carbine sling, with its brass tip and large brass buckle, is worn across his chest. (Mick Kissick)

The Starr carbine, of 0.54 caliber, was similar in design and function to the Sharps; however, its mechanism was more delicate. An ordnance officer reported that "the least dirt deranges it. It requires both hands to press back the lever, the cartridge is not readily placed straight in the barrel, and the gas check is very imperfect. After a few firings the saltpeter corrodes the barrel where it enters the gas check, rendering the level double hard to open. As the part becomes more corroded, the effect of the discharge would be greatly impaired."

The Smith carbine was of 0.50 caliber; it weighed 7fi pounds and was 39 inches long. It was unique among issue carbines, however, in that it used rubber cartridges which sealed the gap in the shotgun-like breech. These cartridges often proved difficult to extract after firing in combat conditions; otherwise, the weapon was fairly popular. Less so

was the 0.52 caliber Cosmopolitan carbine, made in Hamilton, Ohio, of which over 9,000 were acquired by the army during the war. Using linen cartridges, the Cosmopolitan leaked gas on firing, was not sturdy in use, and had inaccurate sights. The Department of West Virginia's Chief Ordnance Officer wrote in August 1864 that the Cosmopolitan was "a very worthless weapon ... thrust upon the Ordnance Department by political influence of contractors."

Only 1,050 Gibbs carbines were issued; this was another weapon that had to be broken open at the breech to allow a linen cartridge to be inserted. A report from an Army of the Potomac ordnance officer dated August 1863 condemned the Gibbs: "I cannot report favorably on the arm. The working is very simple but perfectly exposed rendering it liable to catch all dirt, and the smallest stick or pebble getting into it renders it unserviceable, until it is taken apart and cleaned."

The 0.54 Merrill carbine used a unique top-loading mechanism operated by raising a lever on top of the breech to expose the chamber. A paper cartridge was inserted; when the top lever was closed a small piston pushed the cartridge forward. These weapons, which also came with unique cartridge boxes, were not popular, and were soon replaced in the Eastern theater; after 1863 they were mostly to be found in the West.

Eventually the army turned to carbines which used fixed ammunition that included the primer as well as the powder and round. The 0.54 Burnside used a metallic cartridge otherwise similar to the Smith carbine round. The US government issued more than 50,000 Burnsides, but the troopers were not completely happy with it: the spring holding the lever shut was too weak for prolonged service, and cartridges had a habit of jamming in the breech when the gun was fired.

The Ballard, of which only 1,509 were bought by the US government and 20,000 by the state of Kentucky, used a falling breechblock system including the trigger and hammer, which was lowered to receive the cartridge; after firing a spring-loaded ejecting rod under the breech cleared the weapon for the next round. The 0.5 caliber Maynard used a cartridge with an especially wide base to ease extraction after firing. The cartridge did not contain its own primer, however, and the weapon had to be fired with a standard

musket cap. Though well made and rugged, it saw only little usage in the last years of the war.

Although these carbines used metallic cartridges, which were an improvement over the paper-wrapped rounds so easily destroyed by water or jostling in the cartridge box, they were still loaded and fired one round at a time. Several repeating carbines saw service, and their higher rate of fire gave the Union trooper a definite edge over most opponents. The .52 caliber Spencer was the most popular of these weapons. It used a magazine holding seven rim-fire cartridges in line in a spring-loaded metal tube which was inserted into the butt. It was consequently heavier, at 8¼ pounds empty, although it was only the standard 39 inches long. The army bought over 95,000 Spencers, and they were the most common cavalry weapon by the end of the war.

The Henry rifle, a brass-framed lever-action ancestor of the later famous Winchester, was popular with the troops, who bought many of them privately, but not with the army, which purchased only small numbers. It was never an issued cavalry carbine; at 9¼ pounds and 43½ inches long it was unwieldy for use on horseback, and lacked a rail-

Private Isaac C. Davis, 15th Pennsylvania Cavalry, wearing the dress jacket with the fatigue cap, has an M1851 Colt Navy revolver stuck in his sword belt and an issue cavalry saber at his waist. He holds his Sharps carbine at his side. (John Sickles)

and-ring for attachment to a carbine sling. Nevertheless, a handful of cavalrymen and, especially in the West, mounted infantrymen carried them.

Units formed further West tended to be worse equipped with weapons than those in the East. The 7th Pennsylvania, which served under Generals Rosencrans and Buell in the Western theater, was originally given Belgian muzzle-loading rifles, which were not replaced by Spencer and Burnside carbines until early 1864. The 3rd Colorado, even further west, was formed in August 1864 for a hundred days, largely to fight Indians. Almost two months of that time was wasted in simply acquiring equipment, including weapons, and when the

weapons arrived they were hardly reassuring. "W[e] were armed with old, out-of-date, muzzle-loadin[g] muskets, which were loaded with paper cartridges[,]" recalled one veteran. "We had to tear off the end o[f] the paper cartridge with our teeth, pour the powde[r] into the muzzle of the gun, ram the bullet an[d] paper down on top of the powder, and then see tha[t] the nipple that held the cap was primed befor[e] putting the cap on. These guns carried plenty o[f] powder and lead, but could not be depended on fo[r] accurate shooting except at close range, and it wa[s] slow work reloading them. However, I was fortunat[e] enough to trade my musket for a Sharp's carbine.[”]

US Army Cavalry Weapons

The figures below indicate the numbers of weapo[ns] the US Army acquired and, for the most part, issue[d] between January 1, 1861, and June 30, 1866. Sin[ce]

Weapons Acquired/Issued by US Army Jan. 1, 1861–June 30, 1866

Carbines	Number Acquired	Carbines	Number Acquired
Ballard	1,509	Allen's	536
Ball's	1,002	Adam's	415
Burnside	55,567	Ball's	2,814
Cosmopolitan	9,342	Colt's Army	129,730
Gallagher	22,728	Colt's Navy	17,010
Gibbs'	1,052	Josyln	1,100
Hall's	3,520	Perrin's	200
Joslyn	11,261	Pettingill's	2,001
Lindner	892	Le Faucheux	121,374
Merrill's	14,495	Remington's Army	125,314
Maynard's	20,002	Remington's Navy	11,901
Palmer's	1,001	Raphael's	978
Remington's	20,000	Savage's	11,284
Sharp's	80,512	Starr's	17,952
Smith's	30,062	Roger & Spencer's	5,000
Spencer's	94,196	Whitney	11,214
Starr's	25,603	Foreign	100
Warner's	4,001	Horse pistols	200
Wesson's	151	Signal pistols	348
French carbines	200		
Foreign carbines	10,051		
Musketoons	587		

he period covers some time after the war had ctually ended, it will be skewed toward late-war eapons; for example, vastly more Sharps carbines 1an Spencers were carried in most of the actual avalry combat, particularly in earlier campaigns ich as Shiloh, Antietam, Vicksburg, and ettysburg. Nonetheless, the list shows the roportion of types of weapons Union cavalrymen ctually carried.

FIELD SERVICE

he soldier's day in camp began at dawn, when a ugle call summoned him for the first roll call. 'hereafter the bugle dictated most of his activities, om taking care of the horses to sitting down for inner. Much of the morning, after man and horse ere cared for, was spent in drill, since accurate rill was still considered the prerequisite for all asic battle maneuvers. A dress formation was held 1 the evening, after which the soldier was ismissed and the remaining time, until tattoo, was is own. Sundays were slightly less arduous; a dress arade and full inspection in the morning were ollowed by a free afternoon.

Leisure time was, however, quite rare, as men of 1e 1st Ohio Cavalry soon discovered: "The trooper as his carbine to care for and keep in order, which vens him up with the infantryman in care of arms nd equipments, and in addition to this he has his evolver, saber and horse equipments to keep in rder and his horse to water, feed and groom every ay, and the soldier who enlists in the cavalry rvice expecting a 'soft snap' will soon learn, to his orrow, that he has been laboring under a grievous iistake. On a campaign or march in good weather, hen it is not necessary to pitch tents at night, the fantry stack arms, get supper and are soon at rest r asleep; but not so with the cavalryman – the ompany must first put up the picket rope and then te horses must be watered, fed and groomed. If iere is no forage in the wagon train, he must then unt forage for his horse, and perhaps go a mile or vo for that. Then he unsaddles, gets his coffee, rooms his horse, and is ready to lie down an hour ter the infantryman is asleep. In the morning, if ie cavalry are to move at the same hour the fantry are to march, they must have reveille an our earlier than the infantry, to have time to feed,

Federal Ordnance officers often pulled obsolete equipment out of storage to fill the needs of all the volunteers the army had recruited. This cavalryman holds an M1833 dragoon saber, which was considered too light for field service and was generally unpopular. He has two Colt revolvers stuck in his belt.

groom and water their horses; and while he has the advantage on the march, it would not be considered by the average citizen a very easy task to march forty, fifty or even sixty miles a day mounted, which was a usual occurrence on our scouts and raids."

Discipline

Never the strong point of a volunteer army, discipline loosened further in the field. Foraging to supplement the issued rations was common. Issue rations were both limited and boring: they included desiccated vegetables, a sort of dried soup mix (which apparently consisted mostly of turnips), salt pork or beef, and the infamous "hard tack." Eggs bought or stolen from farmers, and fruit pie from the regimental sutler, brought much-needed variety into the diet.

Stealing was something for which the cavalryman had more frequent opportunities than the infantryman: his duties often took him away from the main body of troops and the prying eyes of superior officers. One Iowa cavalryman noted that many of his mates "carried on a wholesale robbery business. Money, watches, jewelry and valuables of any kind were stolen by them calling themselves forages; they were literally thieves, and robbing banditti." Even when the cavalryman paid for items

from Southern civilians, it was often not with lega currency – a number of enterprising Norther printers produced counterfeit Confederat currency, which they sold cheaply to Union soldier in large quantities.

Sutlers

It was at the training camp that the cavalry recru first met the sutler, one of whom was authorized t each regiment. The sutler was a merchant, who sol products that were not issued by the governmen but were considered important for the soldier health and morale. They worked from a fixed spc in the camp, often a shack with a canvas roof or tent; in the field they operated from wagon According to the exhaustive General Orders No. 2 and 35, dated March 21, 1862, and February 1863, sutlers were authorized to sell: apple oranges, figs, lemons, butter, cheese, milk, syruj molasses, raisins, candles, crackers, wallets, broom comforters, boots, pocket looking glasses, pin

On the move in the field, two cavalrymen shared a single shelter tent, made of two pieces buttoned together. This replicated shelter tent, known by the men as a "dog tent," is ready for inspection, with the occupants' equipment laid out in it.

These cavalrymen, sketched by famous American artist Winslow Homer, enjoy the Thanksgiving holiday in camp at their sutler's tent.

loves, leather, tin washbasins, shirt buttons, horn and brass buttons, newspapers, books, tobacco, cigars, pipes, matches, blacking brushes, clothes brushes, tooth brushes, hair brushes, coarse and fine combs, emery, crocus, pocket handkerchiefs, stationery, armor [gun] oil, sweet oil, rotten stone, razor straps, razors, shaving soap, soap, suspenders [braces], scissors, shoestrings, needles, thread, pencils, belt- and pocket-knives, Bristol brick, canned meats and oysters, dried beef, smoked tongues, tinned and fresh vegetables, pepper, mustard, yeast powders, pickles, sardines, Bologna sausages, eggs, buckwheat flour, mackerel, codfish, poultry, saucepans, tin coffee pots, tin plates and cups, forks, knives, spoons, twine, wrapping paper, uniform clothing for officers, socks, trimmings for uniforms, shoes, shirts and underwear ... In the Western theater sutlers were also allowed to sell bicarbonate of soda, seidlitz powders, yeast powders and even lager beer, though the sale of alcoholic beverages was otherwise generally prohibited.

"Sutlers were regular sharks," wrote one Ohio cavalryman, "and their methods of doing business was by Sutler's checks from one payday to another.

These checks were either tickets or metal representing from ten cents to one dollar, and any soldier could go and get a limited amount of checks and the Sutler would charge him up on his books with the full amount of them, and then when the soldier made his purchases the Sutler would charge him up so as to get at least one hundred percent profit – for instance, fifty cents a pound for cheese, one dollar for a plug of Navy tobacco, and three dollars for a canteen full of commissary whisky, warranted to kill at a hundred yards. When payday arrived the Sutler was on hand at the table besides the Paymaster to collect, and he always got his full share of the greenbacks paid out ..."

In more permanent camps regimental sutlers had fierce competition. Only a short time after arriving at one such camp in early 1862, a New York cavalryman found that outside the bivouac area, "Streets were laid out and named, and long lines of tent-shanties, in which a brisk trade was carried on, gave a [happy] and picturesque appearance to the place. Here a persuasive [merchant] made his bow, and invited you in to buy his cheap clothing and his flimsy haberdashery; there, an enterprising gentleman from Boston had opened a showy establishment, and had everything the soldier wanted, from a bunch of matches to a leathery cheese. Then a respectable-looking gentleman from New York invited you in to see the extensive stock he was just opening, and intended to sell at cost and expenses. He didn't want to make a dollar out of the soldier, he was sure he didn't; and as for the like of a bottle of good whiskey, why he always threw in that as a matter of friendship. The "Broadway Saloon" rivalled with the "Philadelphia House" in the quantity and quality of dinner given you for a dollar. Both had their female contraband [African-American] waiters, draped in the [best] attire; both swarmed with flies, and steamed with the heat of a furnace." On top of all that, it was always possible to find, the cavalryman reported, "a 'little game' going on just beyond the Oaks."

Pastimes

Gambling was always popular: "As soon as the soldiers were paid off, all the little dealers would get out their 'chuck a luck' boards with the mysterious white figures on a black oil-cloth and the games would commence all along the line – in tents, on cracker boxes, on forage sacks and wherever seats could be improvised. In fact, at some points where the troops were paid off there was nothing to buy and nothing to spend money for, and the boys that did not send their money home must spend it in some manner, and in some instances a devotee of the alluring game of 'draw poker' or 'Old sledge' would sit down after being paid off and at one sitting put every dime he had in the 'Jack pot.' But the players were all very liberal, good-hearted fellows, and when a comrade got 'broke' they would always 'put up a stake' for him until the next pay day, if he was 'a square fellow.'"

The same Ohio cavalryman noted that, "In the cavalry service horse racing was the great sport, and the First Ohio was no exception to the rule. When we were in camp for any length of time, and the service was not too hard, the lovers of that sport would improvise a track on some straight stretch of road, or across some old fields or pastures, and the 'sprinters' would be put in training under the care of some experienced horsemen and jockeys, of which there were a number in the regiment ... Very often races would be made with horses of other regiments and the betting would be heavy and the excitement ran high."

One young cavalry bugler rides his animal inside a sutler's tent, while to the left of picture another cavalryman sits on a barrel. The sutler was often the social center of a cavalry camp. (*Frank Leslie's Illustrated News*)

Right: Winter quarters usually consisted of log huts with roofs made from the tents. A company of the 14th Massachusetts Cavalry return to their winter quarters in the winter of 1861–62, while a log-cutting detail, bottom right, chops firewood.

Above: These cavalrymen, seated in front of the camera, look across a camp at a group of some 200 Confederate prisoners captured during the 1862 campaign in the Valley of Virginia. The cavalryman standing, near right, rests on a Sharps carbine. Note the shelter-half tent, open at both ends, on the near left, and the teepee-like Sibley tents, which did not last through the year, on the near right. Shelter-half tents were buttoned together and shared by two men; each Sibley tent was designed to house 20 soldiers and their personal gear, along with a sheet-iron stove in the center for warmth. (National Archive)

Boxes of food, clothing, and reading materials from home were the things that often kept a soldier going. These cavalrymen enjoy one of their fellow troopers' boxes from home during the Christmas 1861 holiday.

Right: Eventually large cash bounties had to be offered to attract recruit into Union cavalry regiments. Here, in the left foreground, a cavalryman tries to persuade a civilian into joining the ranks of his regiment. (*Frank Leslie's Illustrated News*)

With only a limited amount of money available to lose or spend, the soldier had to find some other way of passing most of his idle hours. Wherever possible, the troopers took in the sights; many had seen little of the world beyond their own farms and the nearby small market towns, and cities, especially Washington, were special treats. A visit to the US Capitol building was a must, and many soldiers recorded visits to George Washington's tomb along the Potomac River. Almost everything in the South was of interest, especially the slaves. Few Northerners had seen African–Americans before; and some who had not been in favor of abolition before the war turned abolitionist once they saw how the slaves were forced to live. The averag Union cavalryman, however, is unlikely to hav claimed he was fighting for freedom for the slave or for equality between the races.

Mail writing was very popular – indeed, thanks extensive public schooling in the North, mo soldiers were literate. "Men who never wrote a lette in their lives before, are at it now," wrote a 2nd Ne York Cavalry captain, "those who cannot write at a are either learning, or engage their comrades write for them, and the command is doing mor writing in one day than, I should judge, we used do in a month, and, perhaps, a year." Most of thes letters were predictably similar: they gave new bout the writer, especially his health, and about ther local boys in the same unit; they enquired bout the goings-on back home, especially of nattached women; and they asked for items to be ent from home, including food, stamps (which ere hard to get at the front), items of clothing, nd reading material.

Soldiers also read newspapers sent from home, opular novels (which were cheaply available in aperback), and religious literature, which was idely distributed by chaplains and organizations ch as the Christian Commission. Ambitious men ead military manuals to improve their prospects of romotion. Newspapers from the South could ccasionally be obtained by trade with the enemy.

Fraternization was greatly frowned upon, but hen the two sides went into winter quarters, as ong the Rappahannock River in the winter of 862–63, pickets often held informal truces. ypically, tobacco and newspapers from the onfederates were exchanged for coffee and ewspapers from the Federals. When a river

separated the two sides the men improvised small boats to sail their trading goods across.

Baseball, often called "rounders," was just gaining popularity and was replacing cricket as the most popular American sport. Regiments from largely urban areas where baseball was played, such as New York and Philadelphia, raised teams and taught units from places where the game was still little known. It was a game that could be improvised at short notice; all that was needed was a short pole, easily produced from a young tree, and a ball perhaps made from a walnut wrapped in yarn, with simple markers to indicate bases. A New York cavalryman wrote from camp in early 1862 that "An exciting game of 'baseball' was played on the eleventh, near our camp, between boys of the 'Fourteenth Brooklyn' and the Harris Light [2nd New York Cavalry]. The contest resulted in a drawn game, so that neither could claim the victory."

Concerts put on by various unit bands were another popular form of free entertainment. The same New York cavalryman noted: "To increase the

variety of our experience, and to give it a pleasing tone, Kilpatrick's brigade-band made its first appearance in front of head-quarters this evening. They discourse national airs in a manner that thrilled and elated us, making the welkin ring with their excellent music." Cavalry brigade bands were authorized by General Order No. 91 of July 1861, and were to contain a band leader and 16 musicians. Generally the musicians played some form of brass horn: a cornet (or saxhorn), an alto horn, a tenor horn, a baritone horn, and a bass horn. Drums, both side and bass, and cymbals were occasionally added. In larger bands woodwind sections comprising piccolos, flutes, and soprano clarinets were added, although these were unusual.

Although early in the war the bandsmen were put to work during battle aiding the wounded, this job was later taken over by Ambulance Corpsmen. Bandsmen sometimes reverted to their original role and actually played during battle. During the battle of Dinwiddie Court House, for example, the commanding officer of the 1st Marine Cavalry recalled that "Our band came up from the rear and cheered and animated our hearts by its rich music ere long a rebel band replied by giving us Southern airs; with cheers from each side in encouragement of its own band, a cross-fire of the 'Star Spangled Banner,' 'Yankee Doodle,' and 'John Brown' mingled with 'Dixie' and the 'Bonnie Blue Flag.'"

Religion was an important aspect of life in an age where the majority of the population were churchgoers. Each regiment was authorized a chaplain, though the position was often vacant. Chaplains held religious services on Sundays, and on many other mornings and evenings as well, and these were usually well attended. In many units the men organized their own prayer or Bible study groups, and these were popular whether the unit had a chaplain or not. Chaplains had to be from a recognized Christian faith until the 5th

Americans of the 1860s were often sincerely religious; most Union cavalrymen went to church services when they had the chance. At this one, officers have brought their camp chairs and sit in the front, while a regiment or brigade band, extreme right, plays hymns.

ennsylvania Cavalry Regiment, a unit largely made ¶p of Jews and with a Jewish colonel, appointed a ¶w, Michael Allen, as their chaplain. Allen was a ¶antor rather than a rabbi, although he had ¶ceived a certificate as a *Haber* (Fellow in Jewish ¶udies). Although he was at first dismissed when ¶iscovered by the authorities the rules were ¶anged in 1862, and from then on rabbis were ¶lowed to become chaplains.

Drinking, though officially banned, was always ¶opular. Troops near towns could generally get ¶vay to visit local saloons; otherwise many sutlers ¶neaked liquor into the camps to sell to the troops. ¶eer was not popular at this date except among ¶erman troops, and most men preferred whiskey in ¶ne form or another. Some managed to have ¶iends at home ship them liquor in innocent-¶oking packages – one ingenious man had a bottle ¶nt to him stuffed inside a roast goose. Officers ¶rank wines as well, and often carefully nurtured ¶iendships with the regimental surgeon, who had a ¶pply of whiskey issued for medicinal purposes.

Prostitutes also followed the armies, especially ¶ttling in places such as Washington, where a large ¶umber of troops were in garrison at any given ¶ne. Since the cavalry were often posted on the ¶itskirts of the army they were more able to take ¶lvantage of the available women than the infantry ¶ artillery.

n the March

 great deal of time was spent on the move, ¶owever, where many of these activities were ¶npossible. The cavalry was noted for long marches, ¶oth during campaigns with the rest of the army as ¶ey protected the flanks and scouted ahead, and ¶n raids when they were on their own. Sometimes ¶ey rode for most of the hours of the day and ¶ght. In such cases they often slept in the saddle, ¶rote a 2nd New York Cavalry captain, "either ¶aning forward on the pommel of the saddle, or on ¶e roll of coat and blanket, or sitting quite erect, ¶th an occasional bow forward or to the right or ¶ft, like the swaying of a flag on a signal station, or ¶ke the careenings of a drunken man. The horse of ¶ch a sleeping man will seldom leave his place in ¶e column, though this will sometimes occur, and ¶e man awakes at last to find himself alone with his ¶orse which is grazing along some unknown field ¶ woods. Some men, having lost the column in this

Captain Franklin S. Case, seen here with his wife Clara, was elected second lieutenant of Co. H, 2nd Ohio Volunteer Cavalry when it was formed in August 1861. He was promoted to first lieutenant on May 10, 1862, and to captain on May 19, 1863. Wounded in fighting near Monticello, Kentucky, on June 9, 1863, he was captured at Ream's Station, Virginia, on June 29, 1864. He survived captivity, but his health was so damaged that he was discharged on May 26, 1865; his regiment remained in service until that September. (Sue Kerekgyarto)

way, have fallen into the enemy's hands. Sometimes a fast-walking horse in one of the rear companies will bear his sleeping lord quickly along, forcing his way through the ranks ahead of him, until the poor fellow is awakened, and finds himself just passing by the colonel and his staff at the head of the column!"

When finally able to halt, troops in the field had time to do little more than take care of their horses, cook for themselves, clean their weapons if necessary, and set up shelter-halves or roll up in their waterproofed ponchos and blankets for the night.

COMBAT & TACTICS

Union cavalry was not especially well used in the early days of the war. Most commanders, with backgrounds from other branches of the service, used their cavalrymen on picket or headquarters duty; they were rarely organized into large mobile bodies. As late as 1864, when Maj. Gen. Philip Sheridan assumed command of the Army of the Potomac's Cavalry Corps, this was still often the case. On reviewing his new command he noted that "the horses were thin and very much worn down by excessive and, it seemed to me, unnecessary picket duty, for the cavalry picket line almost completely encircled the infantry and artillery of the army, covering a distance, on a continuous line, of nearly sixty miles, with hardly a mounted Confederate confronting it at any point. From the very beginning of the war the enemy had shown more wisdom respecting his cavalry tha[n] we. Instead of wasting its strength by a policy [of] disintegration he, at an early day, had organize[d] his mounted force into compact masses, an[d] plainly made it a favorite ... "

Eventually, Union commanders took their cu[e] from the Confederacy which, from the beginnin[g] of the war, had grouped its cavalry into fu[ll] brigades and corps and sent them off o[n] destructive raids into enemy territory. By 1863 th[e] lesson had been learned, and the Union se[nt] entire corps of cavalry on raids. Especially notab[le] were Grierson's Raid in April–May 1863 i[n] Mississippi, the strike against Richmond in 186[4,] and Wilson's Raid into Alabama and Georgia i[n] 1865. Indeed, many of the "campaigns" of the wa[r,] such as the 1864 Valley Campaign under Maj. Ge[n.] Sheridan, were really little more than large caval[ry] raids. The objective of these raids was to weake[n] the will of the Southern population to fight, an[d] to destroy the South's agricultural an[d] manufacturing capabilities. This strategy was th[e] cavalry's main contribution to the eventual Unio[n] victory.

Federal cavalrymen capture a Confederate gun near Culpepper, Virginia, on September 14, 1863, following a four–hour–long pitched battle with Confederate cavalry units. (*Frank Leslie's Illustrated News*)

Captain, 1st Dragoons, California 1858

A

Dismounted Saber drill

B

On the march

C

D   A bivouac in the field

Dismounted tactics, Gettysburg, July 1, 1863

E

3

5

6

b

e

2 a

d

c

g

1

4

Private, 1st Ohio

F

Mounted tactics, Yellow Tavern, May 11, 1864

G

The aftermath of battle

H

Live and let live, the Rapidan river, winter 1863-64

I

J   ·The eyes and ears of the army, the Wilderness 1864

Grierson's Raid, Newton Station, Mississippi, April 24, 1863

K

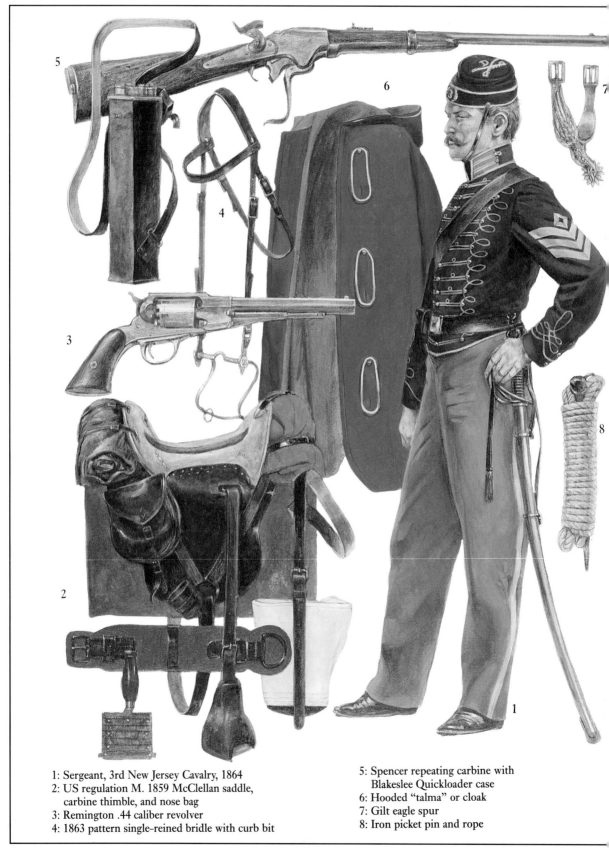

1: Sergeant, 3rd New Jersey Cavalry, 1864
2: US regulation M. 1859 McClellan saddle,
   carbine thimble, and nose bag
3: Remington .44 caliber revolver
4: 1863 pattern single-reined bridle with curb bit

5: Spencer repeating carbine with
   Blakeslee Quickloader case
6: Hooded "talma" or cloak
7: Gilt eagle spur
8: Iron picket pin and rope

L

Deficiencies in tactics

Most recruits believed that cavalry actions would involve hordes of saber-swinging riders dashing on broken infantry formations or against enemy cavalry units, acting like the knights in the books they had read in their childhood. The main cavalry combat doctrine of the time was designed for just such situations; however, in reality combat rarely developed as planned. Foot troops quickly learned that if they remained calm and kept their formations intact no mounted charge could dislodge them. William Watson, of the 3rd Louisiana Infantry, described the first time his regiment met cavalry during the battle of Wilson's Creek: "Suddenly some one cried out that there was cavalry coming down upon us. 'Pooh!' cried Colonel M'Intosh, 'who the devil cares for cavalry? Here, you rifles, take your position along that fence and send them to the rightabout.' This was addressed to our company, and we ran and took up position. We saw the cavalry advancing upon us, but before they came within range of our rifles a shower of grape and shrapnels from Woodruff's battery sent them to the rightabout."

This scene was to be repeated almost every time cavalry attempted to force a dismounted unit's position; as a result, the mounted charge against troops on foot was largely abandoned in practice.

One British professional officer decried Civil War cavalry combat, saying that the saber was rarely used and neither side actually charged the other. Instead, each side would exchange shots, often at fairly safe distances, until one side or the other withdrew. According to a member of the 1st Ohio Cavalry, "in the early part of our service it was usual to halt to receive the attack of the enemy, and attempt to fire from our horses, instead of dismounting to fight on foot, or drawing saber and charging him; all of which we learned before the close of the war."

The reason was simple: modern firearms had made the mounted cavalry charge virtually obsolete. By the time a mounted regiment got close enough to a dismounted unit to engage it with sabers, it had already been torn apart by rifle or carbine fire. In May 1862 a Union cavalry expedition was sent against the Mobile and Ohio Railroad in Missouri. "While we were still wrecking the road," recalled Philip Sheridan, then commander of the 2nd Michigan Cavalry Regiment, "a dash was made at my right and rear by a squadron of Confederate cavalry. This was handsomely met by the reserve under Captain Archibald P. Campbell, of the Second Michigan, who, dismounting a portion of his command, received the enemy with such a volley from his

An artist at the front in fall 1862 sketched this advance of mounted skirmishers from the Army of the Potomac. Advancing on horseback was uncommon; dismounted skirmishing was more usual.

Colt's repeating rifles that the squadron broke and fled in all directions."

In just this way the Union cavalry held up the Confederate advance into Gettysburg on July 1, 1863, long enough for Union infantry to get into a strong defensive position. Indeed, many of Maj. Gen. John Buford's 1st Cavalry Division troopers fought as infantrymen during that action. Some of the 3rd Indiana, for example, had comrades lead their horses to the rear, their carbines still hooked to the saddles; they took up rifled muskets from the fallen, and joined Wisconsin infantrymen from the Iron Brigade. Meanwhile, according to Buford's official report of the battle, other cavalrymen had taken "partial shelter behind a low stone fence, and were in short carbine range. Their fire was perfectly terrific, causing the enemy to break and rally on their second line, which made no further advance toward my position."

This is not to say that the cavalry never charged. Brig. Gen. John Farnsworth led a heroic although costly charge at Gettysburg. On the third day of the battle he was ordered by Army of the Potomac

cavalry division commander Maj. Gen. Judso Kilpatrick to take his brigade across an uneven fie broken by large rocks and small brush, against tw unbroken regiments of Alabama infantry; tw brigades of Confederate infantry on their right als had them in their gunsights. Farnsworth proteste the order, but Kilpatrick, as typically inept as mo early Federal cavalry commanders, insisted on th charge, adding, "If you are afraid to lead th charge, I will lead it." His Victorian sense of hone cut to the quick, Farnsworth demanded th Kilpatrick take back his insinuation, adding that h would indeed lead the charge. He would have bee better advised to take up his superior's offer, for th sake of the lives of many Union cavalrymen who Kilpatrick would waste in the future, if not for h own. The charge did result in the capture of som hundred Confederate infantrymen, but at the lo of 65 good cavalrymen, including Farnswor himself.

Dismounted tactics

Other cavalry units could also handle a sab charge as well as Farnsworth's men; Custe Michigan Brigade, for example, had a reputatio for daredevil assaults. In many cavalry brigad certain regiments or battalions were designated foot units, while others concentrated on the swor

From the time of the organization of the Michigan Brigade," one veteran later recalled, "the First Regiment had been designated as distinctively a saber regiment, the Fifth and Sixth for fighting on foot, as they were armed with Spencer rifles [*sic*], and the result was that with them, dismounting to fight when in contact with the enemy in the early part of their terms became a sort of second nature. The First had a year's experience with the cavalry before the others went out, and it was in a saber charge at the Second Bull Run battle that Brodhead its first colonel was killed. The First Vermont, like the First Michigan, was a saber regiment and went out in 1861. When this regiment was attached to the Brigade, Custer had three saber regiments, and it fell to the lot of the Fifth and Sixth Michigan to be selected more often than the others, perhaps, for dismounted duty. It often happened, however, that the entire brigade fought dismounted at the same time; and sometimes, though not often, all would charge together mounted. Owing to the nature of the country, most of the fighting in Grant's campaign from the Wilderness to the James was done on foot. In the Shenandoah valley campaign in the latter part of the year 1864, the reverse was the case and at the battles of Tom's Brook, Winchester and Cedar Creek the troopers in the command for the most part kept to the saddle throughout the engagements." General Sheridan recalled that his first command contained a "saber battalion," while the rest of the regiment was armed with Colt rifles, which they used as their main weapons.

In such a case, the official tactical system produced by Philip St. George Cooke and published in Philadelphia in 1862, was the first system used. It called for cavalry to deploy in a single line, maneuvering from a column into line by groups of fours. This system did not survive the war. According to a Michigan cavalryman, "The winter of 1863–64 was one of hard work for the Federal cavalry. In addition to their other duties, the Michigan regiments were required to change their tactical formation and learn a new drill. Up to that time Philip St. George Cooke's single rank cavalry tactics had been used. The tactical unit was the set of fours and all movements were executed by wheeling these [four-man] units. There was but one rank. For some reason, it was decided to substitute the old United States cavalry tactics and form in double ranks."

Most fighting, however, was not done according to the manual, on horseback, but dismounted. Each fighting unit retained its four-man basic

This cavalryman posing in front of a Napoleon cannon wears shoulder scales, and an oilcloth rain cover on his cap. A half-chevron on his left forearm indicates that he is a veteran volunteer with three years of Civil War service to his name. (US Army Military History Institute)

component, but in the case of dismounted fighting the fourth man would hold the horses of the other three behind the lines while the three fought the enemy on foot with their carbines.

The range of the carbine largely determined the distances at which cavalrymen fought, and put them at a severe disadvantage when up against enemy infantry. Modern firing tests with US Army issue carbines, conducted by *Gunns & Ammo* magazine with original weapons in excellent condition, rested on sandbags, showed their effective ranges to be significantly less than the longer-barrelled rifled musket of the infantry. An M1861 rifled musket, when shooting offhand, could put ten consecutive shots in an 11-inch bullseye at 333 yards; and it could be sighted and fired at 900 yards. Carbines had sights that allowed for fire at 500 yards, but were not very effective beyond 100 yards. The Sharps, the most common carbine of the war, when fired from a benchrest, placed a group of shots within a five-inch circle at

100 yards; Smith and Merrill carbines were just a accurate. The Spencer, however, could only plac rounds within a seven-inch target at 50 yards and nine-inch one at 100 yards, and was qui inaccurate beyond that range; of course, the seve shot Spencer made up in firepower what it lacke in accuracy.

Successful engagements

The improvements in firepower and range of bo infantry and cavalry weapons dictated radic changes in tactics. Aside from its use in "moppin up" operations, the cavalry charge was virtual defunct; the new tactical emphasis was on mobili and dismounted firepower. This combination wc the day in what may have been the single be example of what the new Union cavalry could do: t capture of Selma, Alabama, by cavalrymen of Ma Gen. James H. Wilson's command in March 1865.

The city was well defended, and fortified depth with a ring of defensive works built by traine engineers months before the assault. Two brigad of dismounted Union cavalrymen armed wi Spencers charged into the defensive lines on foc one group advancing while the other covered the with fire, in a classic alternating fire-and-moveme

Infantry, standing firm, could always drive off cavalry; here Confederates resist a charge of the 5th US Cavalry Regiment during fighting in the Peninsular Campaign, June 27, 1862. An artist for *Harper's Weekly* magazine saw the event and made this sketch of it.

Two guidons are carried in a cavalry charge. The guidon served an actual purpose, both as a point to dress on, and as a rallying point in battle.

aneuver. They rapidly overran an outer line fended by Confederate infantrymen protected by atis. Without a pause, they charged through a cond line 200 yards behind the first, protected by re stretched between low stakes, and sharpened kes sticking out of the ground, and defended by fantry and artillery.

When the dismounted cavalrymen had cleared a p in the second line, mounted troopers charged ough. The 7,000 defenders who had rallied at the ird and final line stopped the mounted charge, so ese cavalrymen dismounted and joined their mrades on foot. The attackers – only 1,700 Union valrymen – quickly forced the final line; then all mounted, and rode quickly into the city. cording to the Confederate commander – the spected Maj. Gen. Natham Bedford Forrest – the eed and momentum of the assault could not be pped. Forrest was under the impression that his en faced equal numbers of attackers, instead of tnumbering them six to one. Union casualties re only 40 killed, 260 wounded, and seven

missing. Confederate casualties are not known, but 2,700 troops and 106 cannons were captured. Wilson himself called it "the most remarkable achievement in the history of modern cavalry, and one admittedly illustrative of its new powers and tendencies."

During the operations of which the capture of Selma formed a part, Wilson's men also made a number of successful night attacks. In one such assault some 400 officers and men of the 3rd Iowa Cavalry captured a Confederate fort near Columbus, Georgia, which was defended by 3,000 Confederates with 27 cannons. At 8.30 p.m. they advanced on foot and brushed aside the defenders; the 10th Missouri Cavalry was sent forward to exploit the success, and although initially successful, the unit was subsequently driven back. The 3rd Iowa then returned to the attack, part

The regulation cavalry company guidon was red, white, and blue, like the US flag, with the company letter in the canton. (West Point Museum Collections)

storming the fortifications under heavy fire; under the cover of darkness much of the shooting was too high, and the dismounted Union troopers soon gained the fort. The rest of the 3rd, which had been kept mounted in reserve, was then sent in to complete the successful capture. Within one hour the battle was over and the fort was in Union hands. There is an unmistakably modern flavor to this action: the Union cavalry exploited speed, firepower, and poor visibility to overcome superior enemy forces.

WOUNDS AND SICKNESS

During the Civil War the prospects for a wounded soldier were not good. Although medical science had made advances over the previous two centuries, it still left a great deal to be desired: the concept of microbes was unknown; instruments and operating areas were not sterilized, and the risk of infection from even minor wounds was extremely high. Rather than the clean slash wounds from sabers which most cavalrymen expected to be the main risk of their branch of service, their most common wounds came in fact from the infantryman's rifled musket and the cavalryman's carbine and pistol: Less than 0.4 percent of all wounds were caused by edged weapons, including bayonets; only 5.5 percent came from artillery, "torpedoes" (mines) and grenades. At Fredericksburg, only six out of the 7,302 recorded Federal wounded were injured by saber or bayonet.

The wounded soldier was first treated by [his] regiment's medical staff, which included a surgeon, an assistant surgeon, and an enlisted hospital steward. The actual job of taking a wounded soldier from the field at first fell to regimental bandsmen. Later in the war enlisted men of the Ambulance Corps, specially appointed and trained and under medical officer supervision, were generally the first to the aid of a stricken soldier. They were usually identified by some special badges, in most armies consisting of a green half-chevron and a band around the cap.

These men brought the soldier to a field aid station, run by the regiment's assistant surgeon and hospital steward. There the wounded were quickly patched up as far as was possible. If the wound was slight, the soldier often opted to return to the front after a short rest; otherwise, he was sent back to the regimental hospital. Here operations such as amputations were performed by the regimental surgeon. Later in the war, however, it was found more efficient to gather all the surgeons from various regiments into a larger hospital organized on a brigade or even division level. Major operations were thereafter generally performed in these hospitals, the best surgeons performing the surgery while the others assisted according to their lights.

If, after a brief stay, the cavalryman was fit to return to his regiment for active duty, he did so. Otherwise he was sent, often in specially equipped railroad hospital cars, to a general hospital in the rear. Most of these permanent hospitals were built around major cities such as Washington, Philadelphia, New York, or Chicago. If he was still unfit for duty after a spell in a general hospital, the trooper was usually discharged, although after early 1863 he could also be transferred for the rest of his period of enlistment into the Invalid Corps (later Veteran Reserve Corps), which performed static guard or provost marshal duties, and helped out in hospitals. Men capable of semi-active duty, who could handle weapons, were assigned to 1st Battalion companies and served mostly as guards, while those who had lost limbs were allotted to 2nd Battalion companies and performed hospital duties.

Bullet wounds were not only the most common battlefield injury they were also the most dangerous. Slow-moving (950 fps muzzle velocity for the infantry rifle musket) and heavy (one ounce), the lead bullets dragged dirty uniform oth and other debris deep into wounds; they shattered bone, and tore flesh. The only way of treating most major wounds to the limbs was amputation. "In the most available places tables have been spread for the purpose of amputations," wrote a New York cavalry officer after Cedar Mountain. "We cannot approach them, with their heaps of mangled hands and feet, of shattered bones and yet quivering flesh, without a shudder. A man must need the highest style of heroism, willing to drag himself or be borne by others to one of these tables, to undergo the process of the amputating blade."

Post-operative infection was always a danger, given the unsanitary operating conditions. Pus was thought, incorrectly, to be a positive sign of recovery; and all too often the black flesh and sickening stench of gangrene followed operations. This mortifying flesh had to be cut away, and secondary amputations were common. A surprising number of men survived both initial and secondary amputations, even if gangrene were involved; blood poisoning, however, was almost always fatal.

There was no planned physical therapy for men to learn to use prostheses in place of their amputated limbs. Men learned to walk again on their own, often with the help of their fellows or others who had previously lost limbs and were now in Veteran Reserve Corps 2nd Battalion companies assigned to the hospital.

Major wounds to the head, chest or abdomen were largely untreatable save by bed care and prayer. Luckily the benefits of operating on unconscious patients had been appreciated almost two decades earlier, and the US Army's medical officers were generally well supplied with anaesthetics such as chloroform.

Living conditions and disease

Huge numbers of men also arrived at hospitals suffering from diseases. Early in the war a great number of soldiers from rural backgrounds fell

At a temporary aid station just behind the front line a regimental assistant surgeon, kneeling left, performs first aid on a patient, while a hospital steward, center, takes medicine out of a specially designed hospital knapsack worn by a soldier assigned for medical service. Here the wounded soldier got the first medical assistance he needed, before being sent on by an ambulance, as in the background, to the regimental or brigade hospital.

prey to basic diseases such as measles, mumps, and chickenpox; they had not been exposed to these ailments in childhood as had soldiers from urban backgrounds. Once in the service, the most common ailments could be traced to microbes in badly cooked food or tainted water. Statistics suggest that the average Union cavalryman was sick twice a year with something major enough to be reported to a doctor. The average mortality rate from these diseases exceeded 53.4 per thousand.

Indeed, the average Civil War soldier was far from aware of the importance of cleanliness in maintaining health. An inspection of the 2nd Iowa Cavalry in January 1862 found "dirty shoes and boots in and about the bunks, [and] scraped sweepings from the floor under the bunks [and tables]." Consequently, while the regiment was in these barracks over 60 of its members died. In the 2nd Michigan Cavalry strict orders were issued that

The large general hospital at Hilton Head, North Carolina, was typical of hospitals built by the army especially for the purpose of receiving and treating large numbers of wounded men. They were designed to admit as much fresh air and light as possible. (*Frank Leslie's Illustrated News*)

straw mattresses and blankets had to be aired f[or] five hours every five days, and the men had to bath[e] "at least once a week," and this regiment lost f[ar] fewer men to disease than did the Iowa uni[t]. Indeed, many regiments had to order their men [to] wash; 1st Massachusetts Cavalry officers had [to] order the troopers to wash their dirty necks, face[s] and hands in January 1863, long after the unit ha[d] been organized.

The South had a far less healthy climate than th[e] northern areas where most of the Union troo[ps] originated. Mosquitoes were common, as we[re] tapeworms and various parasitic microbes. The h[ot] climate itself, especially as experienced in hea[vy] wool uniforms on active service, helped to tire me[n] out and break down their health.

The diseases acquired from unhealth[y] environments were generally treated wit[h] ineffective pharmaceuticals, including mercu[ry]. Alcohol was the primary drug used, although som[e] doctors questioned its use as a general reme[dy]; nonetheless, it was widely dispensed as a fir[st] medicine of choice, which partly explains the lo[ng] lines before the doctor's quarters for daily sick ca[ll]. Quinine was another common drug, as were son[e]

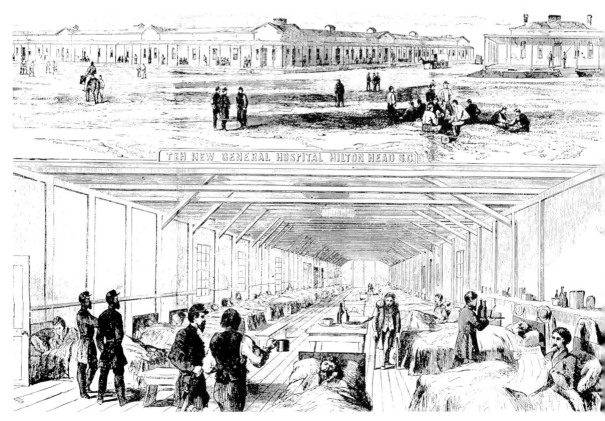

TEH NEW GENERAL HOSPITAL HILTON HEAD S.C.

ystery preparations such as the frequently
entioned "blue mass." The most common
omplaint, diarrhea or dysentery, which averaged
1 per thousand every year, was treated with
psom salts, castor oil (in the morning), or opium
n the evening). Men usually got over the diseases
emselves despite such medicines; however, deaths
om diseases such as chronic diarrhea were not at
l uncommon.

Horses were equally at risk from sickness and
ounds; veterinary science had developed even less
an had medical knowledge. On August 1, 1863,
lowance was made for the appointment of one
eterinary surgeon for each cavalry regiment;
owever, most had little or no actual training. The
w schools in existence varied in quality, and many
ere little more than diploma mills which required
tle education to enter and little more than a
ition "fee" to ensure graduation. Many of these
hools were centered in Philadelphia, where as late
1877 it was possible to purchase a degree in
eterinary science for only $100.

HE PLATES

1: Captain, 1st Dragoons, California, 1858

his officer wears the field dress as laid down in the
357 dress regulations. As this units service in
alifornia had shown in reality many of the items
ould have been modified if not thrown away. In
articular the Jeff Davis or Hardee hat would almost
rtainly have been discarded in favor of a more
actical slouch hat. Many officers replaced the
ock coat with the more comfortable waist length
oth jacket, it is doubtful that the cross belt and
sh would have survived long on active service. The
nit was originally authorized on March 2, 1833, as
e US Regiment of Dragoons but as the cavalry
creasingly developed dismounted tactics the title
Dragoons became superfluous. The unit was
designated as the 1st Cavalry on August 3, 1861.
2: United States Army Cavalry tactics manual; A3:
eld binoculars and case; A4: Stamped brass
valry officer's badge; A5: Officers' and NCOs' belt
uckle; A6: Dragoon tunic button; A7: Enlisted
an's waist belt. Buff-leather with brass keeps, and
andard belt-plate; A8: Model 1860 .44-caliber Colt
rmy revolver, widely issued to cavalrymen, taking
ose powder and ball or cartridges of paper, foil, or

The cape on the mounted man's overcoat reached well below
the wrists. (Richard Carlile Collection)

skin; A9: Standard issue cavalry spur; A10: Pistol
ammunition, .44-caliber Colt paper cartridges that
required percussion caps which would have been
carried in a cap box on the waist-belt.

B: Dismounted saber drill

The only way to familiarize the raw recruits with the
confusing array of weapons and equipment was
repetitive drill. They would invariably arrive at their
units with little or nothing in the way of training. If
there was a lull in the fighting then there might be

time enough for a more experienced NCO to teach them some basic skills. If the unit was on campaign however they would have to learn "on the job," which might make the difference between life and death. Here a corporal is taking the opportunity of a break on the march to introduce three recruits to the mysteries of the saber. The middle trooper has correctly adopted position 41, right point. His comrades have not performed quite as well. The trooper on the right has in fact adopted position 55, against infantry right parry, although he may just have realized his error. Their companion seems to be struggling but he may well never get to use the saber in anger anyway. The carbine was rapidly becoming the trooper's preferred weapon, the increased accuracy and effectiveness of firearms and artillery having rendered the old–fashioned cavalry charge practically suicidal. Judging by the amused looks of the old sweats in the background this is a lesson they have already learned.

C: On the march

During the early years of the war the Federal cavalry lacked the confidence and experience to cut loose from its large, slow–moving field armies in the wa that the Southern troopers seemed able to d almost at will. Their duties were largely confined those of headquarters guards and courier although they were still expected to provide protective screen around the army to discourag the enemy's inquisitive scouts. When on campaig they would more often than not have bee encumbered with all the impedimenta of th logistic "tail" of the army. This lack of mobility ar confidence greatly reduced the effectiveness of th cavalry arm in the early years of the war.

D: A bivouac in the field

Conditions on campaign were spartan for a concerned but particularly so for the rank and fil The enlisted trooper would often share a two-ma button-down canvas tent, or if encamped for period of time and well supplied might have th

Cavalry means horses, which therefore requires the equipme to keep them in the field. The blacksmith and his portable forge was an important figure in the cavalry regiments. (*Fran Leslie's Illustrated News*)

ight comfort of living in a 20–berth "Sibley" tent. ven under the best of circumstances conditions ere cramped, and he still had the major task of king care of his main asset, his horse.

The officers on the other hand did have some egree of comfort, always allowing for a lull in the ghting or a rest period. They usually had a tent r themselves where some of the comforts of home ight be stowed away as we see in this scene.

writing desk and stationery set were always easured items, for letters home and for the orders f the day. He may well have had, depending pon rank, an array of personal possessions such traveling chest; portable stove; drinks cabinet; ie current newspapers; and a fresh supply of ooks. If the unit was traveling light, however, ie officers would often be expected to tolerate ie same conditions as the men under their ommand.

: Dismounted tactics, Major General John uford's 1st Cavalry Division, Gettysburg, July , 1863

They will attack you in the morning and they will me booming. . . You will have to fight like the devil ntil support arrives." John Buford's prediction to ue of his brigade commanders the night efore the Battle of Gettysburg emphasized the ile his cavalry corps would play in this ngagement. They met the advance of Heth's labama and Mississippi divisions head on as they ade their way up the Chambersburg Pike, north est of Gettysburg heading toward the town, xpecting to meet little resistance from the Federal avalry detachment they knew to be there. Buford, strong–willed Kentuckian regular soldier and ex- ıdian fighter, commanded a tightly disciplined ıd experienced corps of troopers. An added dvantage was their newly equipped seven-shot harps carbine which in the hands of a sound ıarksman could loose off 20 rounds per minute. 'ith five times the fire power of the "Butternut" oldiers advancing toward them they presented formidable barrier.

This was classic dismounted tactics; one out of our remained in the rear holding the horses whilst

the other three engaged with their carbines and pistols from behind the small stone wall. Buford's two dismounted brigades, after two hard hours of heavy fighting, managed to hold the ridge until reinforced in the nick of time by General Reynolds's infantry, thus saving the Union left flank from collapse at such an early stage of the battle.

FI: Private, 1st Ohio

This trooper typifies the rugged western Yankees who entered service as "horse soldiers." Tough,

his double-breasted regulation field grade officer's coat was orn by Lieutenant Colonel Augustus W. Corliss, 2nd Rhode land Cavalry. (Chris Nelson)

lean and with very few of the frills that one would expect from the dashing beaux *sabreurs* of the eastern states.

They were similar to their southern counterparts in that they too came from a mainly rural background and thus did not have trouble familiarizing themselves to horse culture or the rigors of that lifestyle. Equipped with the basic essentials of carbine, pistols, and saber they were a real handful for all opposition they faced.

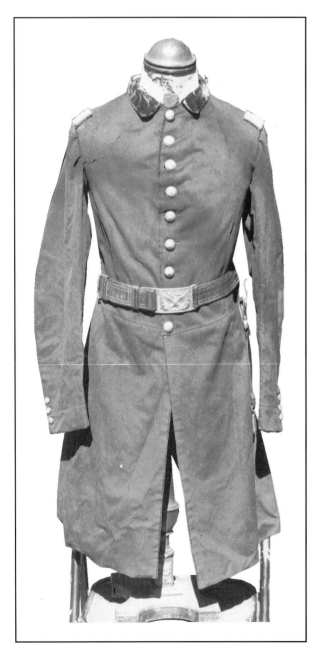

Dressed in regulation dark blue tunic, sky blu[e] trousers and wearing the casual slouch hat tha[t] many preferred, this trooper has the Burnsid[e] carbine attached to a shoulder belt, making it fa[r] easier to handle once on horseback. He woul[d] always carry normally at least one pistol and h[is] saber, although the latter was sometimes dispense[d] with. F2(a): Knapsack, usually leather an[d] containing personal belongings; (b): playing card[s] (c): cut-throat razor; (d): Bible; (e): tobacco pip[e] (f). watch; (g): canteen; P3: Burnside carbine; F[?] carbine sling with attachment device; F5: carbin[e] cartridge box with belt loops; F6: cartridge an[d] percussion caps.

G: Mounted tactics, Yellow Tavern, May 11, 1864

By this stage of the war the Federal cavalry uni[ts] were more than capable of "mixing it" with the[ir] southern counterparts. This was demonstrate[d] when Sheridan's troopers engaged arguably th[e] finest cavalry force in the Confederacy, at Yello[w] Tavern. While on a raid into the rear areas [of] General Lee's Army of Northern Virginia the[y] encountered Jeb Stuart's southern horsemen [a] mere six miles from Richmond. This was a typic[al] mounted cavalry encounter, repeated sweepin[g] charges at the enemy using pistols, carbines, an[d] sabers.

Stuart was in the thick of the action, as was h[is] habit, showing the fearless bravado and dash tha[t] his troops loved, and enemies respected. He carrie[d] for close-quarters fighting his Whitney revolver, [a] most effective weapon for any cavalryman when i[n] the thick of a full–blooded melee. Stuart himself wa[s] mortally wounded in the right side by a single .4[?] caliber ball fired by a private (who himself wa[s] killed eleven days after this event). Stuart died [2] hours later.

By 1864 the Union cavalry were in th[e] ascendance, with new weaponry and healthy horse[s] and the confidence in their ability to use the[m] successfully. They also learned from th[e] Confederate cavalry and their own experience, ho[w]

This version of the company grade officer's coat was worn by Captain John Hobensack, 1st New Jersey Cavalry. The collar has been turned down and shows its black velvet lining. The sword belt is an officer's version, with a brass buckle used to adjust the waist size on the right hip. (Chris Nelson)

est to hurt their enemy and how to be best used as
force for quick and decisive actions. It would be
heridan's cavalry corps who would speed the
estruction and defeat of the Confederates with
urious raids on their industrial bases, and the
arassing and cutting off of their army's supply
nes, trapping General Lee and the remnants of his
eleaguered force at Appomattox Station on April
, after their defeat at the Battle of Five Forks seven
ays earlier. Thus bringing the war to an end.

: The Aftermath of battle

he horrors of the war are best witnessed after a
attle," stated a Vermont sergeant who had seen his
ir share of fighting, and indeed the treatment
ceived once wounded was marginal until one
ached a medical unit. Even then basic errors in
ow to combat the spread of disease and infection
d many men to suffer the dreaded consequence
f amputation, or death from peritonitis,
eningitis and other transmitted diseases picked
p from the unsterilized surgeons' hands and their
struments. Over 90 percent of all Civil War
ounds were caused by the rifle bullet, their low
locity resulting in smashed limbs and severed
teries, which were an open invitation to infection
not treated immediately. Such was the use of large-
liber ammunition such as the .75, that a wound to
e abdomen or the chest was fatal.

For the cavalry trooper often involved in
irmishes far ahead of the main column of the
my, or on deep penetration raids into enemy
rritory, receiving first aid was a major concern.
ven with the fighting continuing further afield
om this scene, casualties expected to receive only
asic treatment before they were transported to a
eld hospital. The wounded and dying had to rely
n their comrades or front-line orderlies to care for
em, which was basic first aid, whilst the battle still
ged.

Live and let live, the Rapidan river,
inter 1863-64

lthough officially forbidden, this sort of
aternization was common with both sides swapping

everything from coffee and food, to newspapers and
tobacco. During a lull in the fighting and
particularly in winter, unofficial truces would be
agreed between units facing each other and a modus
vivendi established that would cause the least
discomfort for each. Once campaigning began both
sides would take up the fight in earnest, however.

It is noticeable the disparity in quality in clothing
and provisions between the combatants; the
Confederates wearing a rag-tag mixture of southern

rst Lieutenant William Schmalz, 5th West Virginia Cavalry,
ears the plain waist-length jacket often preferred to the frock
at for mounted use. He has also acquired a pair of dark
ather gloves for riding. (David Scheinmann)

uniforms which they have collected on their travels, whilst their Federal counterparts are kitted out in relatively new uniforms and winter overcoats. The Union always enjoyed a monopoly on materials and supply and by this stage of the war far exceeded the South in clothing, feeding, and arming its troops and population.

J: The eyes and ears of the army, the Wilderness, 1864

The cavalry were the antennae of the army, helping the ponderous bulk of the main force seek out the enemy. Through scouting and reconnaissanc[e] they would feel their way around the opposin[g] force, monitoring movements, gatherin[g] information and assessing its weak points. Pa[rt] of their role was to observe the enemy withou[t] being discovered themselves. By pinpointin[g] which units were moving and to where the[y] could help determine where the Confederat[es] would strike next. By the latter part of the war th[e] Federal cavalry had developed not only th[e] confidence but the skill and subtlety to excel in th[is] role.

K: Grierson's Raid, Newton Station, Mississippi, April 24, 1863

In the last two weeks of April 1863, General Gra[nt] was endeavoring to bring his army within strikin[g] distance of Vicksburg. He ordered Colon[el] Benjamin H. Grierson south into the Mississippi t[o] attack and destroy Pemberton's communicatio[n] and supply lines, to stir up as much alarm a[s] possible and to distract the Confederates whi[le] Grant moved his forces across the river belo[w] Vicksburg thus out-flanking the city's defense[s]. Heading a 1,700-strong force (protected by forwa[rd] recce scouts known as the "Butternut Guerrilla[s]" due to their disguised rebel attire to avoi[d] discovery) Grierson would cover over 600 miles [of] road and swamp destroying Confederate ordnanc[e,] railroad track and supplies between Vicksburg an[d] Mobile. Continually harassed by militia units, an[d] pursued by a larger force of regular Confedera[te] troops, the blue raiders successfully complete[d] their mission in sixteen days arriving safely [at] Baton-Rouge. They had killed or wounded 1[00] Confederates, captured and paroled 500 more, to[re] up 50 miles of rail track and captured 1,000 hors[es] and mules (Grierson's losses were three kille[d,] seven wounded and nine missing), leaving Gener[al] Sheridan to describe it as "... the most brillia[nt] expedition of the war."

On April 24 they entered Newton Station, [a] track-side hamlet 25 miles west of Meridan, whic[h] had been seized earlier in the day by the "Butter[nut]

Colonel James B. Swain, 11th New York Cavalry, wears a lamb's-wool-trimmed jacket; this style was very popular amon[g] mounted officers. Swain, a poor officer, was court-martialed o[n] a number of charges in February 1864, and dismissed from th[e] service that month. (Benedict R. Maryniak)

uerrillas" and was now in the process of being destroyed. Two locomotives were wrecked, along with over 30 freight cars loaded with supplies for Vicksburg. Other details of men are ripping up track, burning sleepers, tearing down telegraph wires, and setting fire to a government building housing caches of small arms. By 2 o'clock the action was complete and the column moved onwards further south leaving their morning's work smoldering away behind them.

Sergeant, 3rd New Jersey Cavalry, 1864

Although toward the war's end the Federal cavalry were equipped and supplied via centralized depots there were still units who stood out as belonging to another time or place. One such regiment was the 3rd New Jersey Cavalry, or the "Butterflies," a nickname they earned for their flamboyant attire. Raised initially in January 1864 as the 1st US Hussars they were dressed in such splendor previously unseen in other Federal cavalry regiments, in an attempt to attract new recruits. Yet their appearance as almost "toy

soldiers" was very deceptive, as they were the embodiment of what the Union cavalryman had become by 1865; heavily armed with repeating Spencer carbines and .44 Remington revolvers which gave them the edge in skirmishes and melees with rebel cavalry and infantry units alike.

The state paid for the additions to the regulation cavalry uniform; the cap was the issue forage cap with peak removed, extra braid was placed on the jacket, and the remainder US Army regulation. This regiment was typical of the new "horse soldier" serving under General Sheridan they no longer merely served as a screen for advancing infantry. Possessing tremendous firepower and with the ability to hit the enemy hard and fast they had evolved into a powerful force capable of independent action.

The 3rd New Jersey would serve with distinction until the war's end routing southern cavalry at Tom's Brook, Virginia; and seeing action at the Battle of Five Forks, which helped force Lee's battered army out of its fortifications around Petersburg.

59

SITES OF INTEREST

Antietam National Battlefield Site, Sharpsburg, Maryland

Site of the single bloodiest day of the war, the visitor center features one of the best short films made on the war and is worth the visit for that alone. There is also a collection of militaria, including weapons, uniforms, medical equipment, ammunition, and provisions.

Carlisle Barracks, Carlisle, Pennsylvania

Established as a military post in 1757, Carlisle Barracks was the site of the School of Cavalry Practice from 1838 until 1861. Regular army cavalry recruits were trained here during that time, as were local volunteer units at the outbreak of the war. The Barracks were captured and burned by Confederate cavalry, June 27–29, 1863, and most of the buildings are of later date; but Quarters 2 and the Hessian powder magazine survived the fire, and the Coren Apartments (officers' quarters) were rebuilt immediately after the fire to original specifications. Today the Barracks house the US Army Military History Institute library and collection.

Carter House Military Museum, Franklin, Tennessee

The Carter House was in the center of the defending Union line at Franklin, while the cavalry served on the flanks of the battle. Maps in this private museum show the unit positions well, while the collection includes a fine variety of weapons, uniforms, and documents. Although now an antiques- and crafts-centered village, the town is outwardly little changed since the battle.

Cedar Creek, near Strasbourg, Virginia

Here Union cavalry commander Philip Sheridan and one of his leading subordinates, George A. Custer, had one of their finest moments. Belle Grove Plantation house still looks much as it did during the battle when it was Sheridan's headquarters, as does much of the battlefield.

Chickamauga – Chattanooga National Military Park, Fort Oglethorpe, Georgia

The largest national military park, with some 8,000 acres; the highlight of the visitor center is the Fuller Gun Collection, which contains a wide variety of cavalry as well as other US Civil War shoulder arms.

Fort Chickamauga, Cookson, Oklahoma

Run by the Sons of Veterans Reserve, an organization of those descended from Union soldiers, Fort Chickamauga is the only horse cavalry post still active in the US. Its activities are largely centered on the years just after the Civil War, but many of the "living history" activities are also relevant to 1861–65.

Fort Donelson National Military Park, Dover, Tennessee

Not really a cavalry battle site; nonetheless the park visitor center does contain a wide variety of wartime artifacts, many of which pertain to the US cavalry.

Fredericksburg and Spotsylvania National Military Park, Fredericksburg, Virginia

The center for parks on the sites of four major actions – Chancellorsville, Fredericksburg, the Wilderness, and Spotsylvania Court House – the museum has an excellent weapons collection as well as a variety of unusual uniforms and related objects.

Gettysburg National Military Park, Gettysburg, Pennsylvania

The site of one of the greatest battles ever fought in North America, which started with Buford's cavalry fight of July 3, 1863. The excellent museum has a wide variety of artifacts relating to the Union cavalry, including weapons, uniforms, and equipment.

Manassas National Battlefield Park, Manassas, Virginia

Site of two major battles, in 1861 and 1862, the headquarters houses both an excellent museum and a top-grade research library. The latter includes a number of important manuscript collections, including the papers of Generals J.B. Ricketts and Fitz-John Porter.

Mansfield State Commemorative Area, Mansfield, Louisiana

A private park just south of Mansfield; the museum contains material on the Red River Campaign, along with a collection of uniforms, weapons, and artifacts. It also houses an extensive and interesting Civil War library.

ea Ridge National Military Park, Pea idge, Arkansas

ite of the most important battle to have een fought in Arkansas, ten miles northeast f Rogers, the area is still relatively untouched. he visitor center contains a collection of eapons, uniforms, and displays, and eplicated equipment shows how the items were sed.

etersburg National Battlefield

nion cavalry did play an important part in the ghting during the siege, which lasted from June 864 until April 1865. The museum at the visitor enter takes due note of the fact, with displays of avalry artifacts.

hiloh National Military Park, Shiloh, ennessee

he museum at the visitor center on this 1862 attlefield includes a number of items of cavalry iterest including pistols, carbines, sabers, boots, vord-belt plates, and uniforms.

Stones River National Battlefield, Murfreesboro, Tennessee

The visitor center contains a section on cavalry which includes weapons and incidental items such as spurs.

US Cavalry Museum, Fort Riley, Kansas

Located in the traditional home of the US Army's cavalry, the museum contains weapons, uniforms, and cavalry equipment, including a large variety of issue saddles. The library is stocked with useful books, maps, early training films, and other reference materials.

War Library and Museum, Philadelphia, Pennsylvania

Organized by a veteran officers' group, the Military Order of the Loyal Legion of the United States, the museum has a number of interesting cavalry guidons, weapons, and uniforms. The building also houses an extensive Civil War library, with one of the best collections of unit histories in the country.

e US flag, Hollywood ovies notwithstanding, as not authorized for valry use. However, any volunteer units tained variations of it. is particular example, rried by the 22nd nnsylvania Cavalry, d the seal of the mmonwealth of nnsylvania painted in e canton as well as the ars. (Pennsylvania pitol Preservation mmittee)

West Point Museum, US Military Academy, West Point, New York

One of the world's leading military museums, the collection includes paintings, flags, uniforms, weapons, and edged weapons. Much of the emphasis is on the Civil War, although displays are changed from time to time.

BIBLIOGRAPHY

"A Cavalryman" (F. Colburn Adams) *A Trooper's Adventures in the War for the Union*, New York, 1895

George W. Adams, *Doctors in Blue*, New York, 1961

Samuel Bates, *History of the Pennsylvania Volunteers, 1862–1865*, Harrisburg, Pennsylvania, 1869

Heros von Borcke, *Memoirs of the Confederate War for Independence*, New York, 1938

William M. Breakenridge, *Helldorado*, Chicago, 1982

Franklin L. Burns, "Sergeant Harry Burns and the 7th Pennsylvania Volunteer Cavalry," *Tredyffrin Easttown Historical Club Quarterly*, Vol. XXIV, No.1

Earl J. Coates and Dean S. Thomas, *An Introduction To Civil War Small Arms*, Gettysburg, Pennsylvania, 1990

Philip St. George Cooke, *Cavalry Tactics: or, Regulations for the Instruction, Formations, and Movements of the Cavalry of the Army and Volunteers of the United States*, Philadelphia, 1862

W.F. Curry, *Four Years in the Saddle*, Columbus, Ohio, 1898

Williard Glazier, *Three Years in the Federal Cavalry*, New York, 1874

Samuel L. Gracey, *Annals of the Sixth Pennsylvania Cavalry*, Philidelphia, 1868

Group 94, National Archives Washington

August V. Kautz, *Customs of the Service*, Philadelphia, 1864

J.H. Kidd, *Personal Recollections of a Cavalryman*, Ionia, Michigan, 1908

John H. Martin, *Columbus, Geo., from its Selection as "Trading Town" in 1827 to its Partial Destruction Wilson's Raid in 1865*, Columbus, Georgia, 1874

Frank Moore, ed, *The Rebellion Record: A Diary American Events*, New York, 1868, Vol.II

H.P. Moyer, *History of the Seventeenth Regiment Pennsylvan Volunteer Cavalry*, Lebanon, Pennsylvania, 1911

Original Documents in the author's collection

ORs, Series I, Vol, XXVII, Part I

ORs, Series III, Vol. III

George W. Peck, *How Private Geo. W. Peck Put Down Rebellion*, Chicago, 1887

Lyman B. Pierce, *History of the Second Iowa Caval* Burlington, Iowa, 1865

Henry R. Pyne, *Ride to War, The History of the First Ne Jersey Cavalry*, New Brunswick, New Jersey, 1961

John W. Rowell, *Yankee Cavalryman*, Knoxvill Tennessee, 1971

Second Iowa Volunteer Cavalry, Regimental ar Company Order and Letter Books, Record

Philip Sheridan, *Civil War Memoirs*, New York, 1991

Stephen Z. Starr, "Hawkeyes On Horseback," *Civil W History*, September 1977, Vol. 23, No.3

Steven Z. Starr, *The Union Cavalry in the Civil W* Baton Rouge, Vol. I, Louisiana, 1979

James H. Stevenson, "The First Cavalry," *The Annals the War*, Dayton, Ohio, 1988

Edward P. Tobie, *History of the First Maine Caval 1861–1865*, Boxton, 1887

The War of the Rebellion: A Compilation of Official Records of the Union and Confederate Armi Washington, Series III, Vol.I

William Watson, *Life in the Confederate Army*, New York, 188

State cavalry regiments often carried versions of their state flag instead of the regulation US cavalry color. This particular example bears the arms of Pennsylvania, and was carried by the 17th Cavalry Regiment of that state. (Pennsylvania Capitol Preservation Committee)

INDEX

Figures in **bold** refer to illustrations